A HILL FARMER'S YEAR

A HILL FARMER'S YEAR

IAN ALCOCK
Illustrated by Rodger McPhail

SWAN·HILL
PRESS

Copyright © 1995 by Ian Alcock (Text)
          © 1995 by Rodger McPhail (Illustrations)

First published in the UK in 1995 by Swan Hill Press
an imprint of Airlife Publishing Ltd

British Library Cataloguing in Publication Data
    A catalogue record for this book
    is available from the British Library

ISBN 1 85310 489 2

Typeset by Hewer Text Composition Services, Edinburgh
Printed in England by Livesey Ltd, Shrewsbury

Swan Hill Press

an imprint of Airlife Publishing Ltd
101 Longden Road, Shrewsbury SY3 9EB

Author's Preface

Mention a farm to most people and they will form a picture of extensive fields of cereal crops, huge expensive-looking machinery, dazzling yellow acres of sickeningly sweet-smelling oilseed rape, and so on. If they think of animals it will probably be of barley-fed cattle, intensive pig units, battery hens or dairy herds. The majority of urban dwellers may have little idea that there are several thousand hill farms where the land is farmed in a more traditional way. A few visitors and tourists to hill country will see these small farms, but when they peer over the dyke or picnic in a gateway, or walk across the fields, they doubtless imagine the 'good life' of the farmers, giving little thought to the fact that the fields are not always green, the birds are not always singing, and the lambs that they see gambolling are the ones that survived. They do not see the pitiful pile of dead lambs in the burial hole, or the farmer struggling to help deliver a calf that is coming the wrong way round, or the rabbits spoiling the fields, or the shepherd battling to feed his ewes in mud and snow. They are unlikely to appreciate that the farmer leaning on the gate looking at his cows, or walking amongst the ewes, is doing so with an eye more critical than that of any welfarist, alert for any signs of ill health or unusual behaviour. The animals cannot report sick, and the farmer has to be vigilant for any sign of discomfort.

The hill farmer mostly works long hours, on call all the time; for animals do not recognize holidays or days of rest. Many hill farmers have never had a holiday, and would not want one even if they could afford it. Some may never have been out of the county in which they have lived all their lives. The urban dweller knows little of the often tiring and dirty work involved in stock farming; or of the occupational diseases such as brucellosis, Lyme disease, farmer's lung, or the health risks of chemicals such as sheep dips, for which there are no known cures if discovered too late. Most hill farmers are exposed to these hazards from which a high proportion suffer.

But the hill farmer is nothing if not an optimist, and does not care to dwell too much on the less pleasant side of farming, for if he did he would surely not continue a way of life that earns him a living that most urban dwellers would consider to be derisory. As the song says 'Money have I none; but I have silver in the stars, and gold in the morning sun!' So those farmers with the eyes to see and the ears to hear can reap the rewards that nature has to offer for tending the land. Without the hill farmer and his grazing livestock many of the flower-rich meadows would disappear into scrub and rushes, and many familiar nesting birds would lose their breeding grounds, and the disappearance of hill flocks and herds would mean the end of the source of the country's best quality meat, wool and leather. Hill farming is a job as well as a way of life, but is one that is more dependent upon the seasons and the weather than most others.

The Farmer's Toast

Let the wealthy and great
Roll in splendour and state,
I envy them not, I declare it.
I eat my own lamb,
My own chicken and ham,
I shear my own fleece and I wear it.

I have lawns, I have bowers,
I have fruits, I have flowers,
The lark is my morning alarmer,
So jolly boys now,
Here's God speed the plough,
Long life and success to the Farmer!

March

Most people celebrate the start of a new year at the beginning of January, the first month of our calendar; but the origins of this were not the marking of another year but rather a midwinter feast held at the halfway point of the long, dreary winter period of hunger and cold. At this point too, no doubt stock was taken of the food supplies to ensure that there was sufficient to see the people through the rest of the winter.

For the hill farmer January is not even half-way through the winter, since although this may be the case in lower country further south, in the hills the worst of the winter is yet to come. The bad weather often comes in January and February, and March is the hungry period when most of the winter keep and rough grazing has gone and it is still a long time before new growth starts again for feeding the animals.

Hill farmers are livestock farmers, mostly because their land is not suitable for growing crops. What ground is available as fields is often too steep for normal cultivation, or too uneven or stony. They may have a few fields near the farm where they can grow some hay, or a field of oats or barley, as winter food for their animals, but mostly their farming involves keeping cattle and sheep.

In the rich farmlands in the south, where winter is more gentle and spring comes early, lambing is probably well under way in March, and perhaps even already over, but in the hills bad weather continues into April. The returning 'teuchat' (the local name for the green plover, peewit or lapwing) often heralds the arrival of the 'teuchat storms' in late March and early April, and heavy rain and sleet can kill new lambs with hypothermia overnight. The weather can still be bad in April, but by then the days are starting to grow noticeably longer and the temperature kinder, and that is the month when most hill farmers start their lambing, which is determined by the date in autumn when the tups or rams are put in with the ewes.

By March the ewes are starting to look heavy in lamb and need both careful attention and extra feeding. In the last few weeks before birth the lambs start to put on significant weight inside their mothers, and the ewes need extra nourishment to feed the growing lambs as well as to not only maintain their own condition, but to render them fit for the effort of lambing and for producing sufficient milk for the lambs after they are born. Most hill farmers start feeding the ewes extra high protein food four to six weeks before lambing is due. Not all the sheep lamb at once, of course, so for some of the later lambers the feeding period will be much longer, since the farmer has to cater for all and cannot feed them individually. In some of the high hill areas, where sheep have to graze large areas of moorland or bare hillsides in order to find sufficient to eat, they tend to be much wilder and in many cases these flocks do not come in to be fed. The result is that a significant number of these ewes either lose their lambs soon after birth or do not lamb at all and the lambing percentages are low. In rough country a single lamb is often preferable to twins, being more likely to survive with its mother's undivided attention and milk supply. In less wild areas, where perhaps the ewes can be brought into the fields near the farmhouse before lambing time for extra attention, the farmer or shepherd would hope to average perhaps 125 to 150 lambs born to 100 ewes, with most of these being raised to saleable age but in hill country a lambing percentage of 90 per cent or less may be the best that can be hoped for, and in some high country the farmer may have to be satisfied with a figure as low as 70 per cent. This compares to a lambing percentage of at least 200 per cent, and sometimes more, that might be expected in lowland flocks in the south.

Although lambing time is traditionally the most traumatic part of the shepherd's year, often many of the problems and casualties arise in the week or two before lambing starts. The rapid growth of the lamb inside the ewe, and the extra weight of the lamb and its associated fluids and membranes, put great pressure upon the sheep, not only from the nutritional viewpoint but also from the purely physical business of moving around normally. At this time of year the farmer and shepherd have to be very watchful for problems and for sheep that do not look well.

In March the hills are bare, the rough vegetation has been grazed down by the cattle and sheep or withered away by the winter weather. This is a hungry time of year for outwintered stock looking forward hopefully to the new growths of spring that are still weeks away from materializing. The cattle are waiting each morning at their feeding place for bales of hay to be put into the haiks (containers made of mesh or metal bars) for their daily feed or spread upon the ground for them, and glad of the opportunity to lick supplementary feed blocks and salt licks put out into containers. The beasts jostling round this food churn up the ground into thick mud in damp weather and they have to be moved regularly to firmer ground, or the tractor would be unable to reach them through the mud, and trampling through thick *glaur* is not good for the cattle. Much of the hill farmer's morning may be taken up with feeding cattle and sheep, particularly if adverse weather conditions such as ice and snow make it difficult to drive about in the tractor.

Where the cattle have a degree of shelter from the wind, under trees or behind clumps of tall gorse for example, most of the hardy indigenous breeds and their crosses winter better outside in the clean fresh air where they are well able to withstand cold temperatures and have plenty of excercise. Whereas inside buildings in the warm damp atmosphere created, even when there is good ventilation, the animals live in close proximity to each other and consequently are susceptible to a number of diseases. This applies particularly to young calves.

It is the same for sheep of course. The modern tendency is to lamb ewes inside buildings, but this procedure does have problems. For most hill farmers inside lambing is impractical, partly because of the extensive range of their ewes and partly because sufficiently large buildings are rarely available. Animals that are used to living outside, especially if they grow winter coats, do not care to be in closed buildings, and are susceptible to diseases resulting from inadequate ventilation, or picked up from bedding, or from close proximity to other sheep. When sheep are lambed inside a building, careful watch has to be kept because several ewes lambing at once with more than one lamb each, and especially with multiple births, can get into confusion over the possession of lambs that may be difficult to sort out. For this reason lambing inside can often be more work over a short period than outside lambing. Most small hill farmers lamb their flocks outside in fields near to the house, where they can be watched and checked several times a day. This procedure starts in March for April lambing ewes together with the feeding of concentrates and hay. In bad weather the sheep may have been given hay already during the winter, but it is as lambing approaches that adequate feeding for the fast-growing embryo lambs becomes important.

Sheep and cattle soon get used to being fed, and after the first few mornings of calling the ewes down to the troughs they are generally waiting nearby, or come running at the sound of the tractor. If there is clean, dry turf on which to put the feed, and enough space to vary the feeding spot daily, it is often easier to put the concentrates straight onto the ground if these are in cob or cake form. Then one can run along with the bag spreading the feed in a long line. If you watch lambs or calves coming to suckle their dam you will notice that the young animal goes round in front of its mother to stop her, and then comes alongside to suckle. This instinct remains with the animals, and, as a result, the instinct of the sheep when you have a bag of feed is to run round in front of you. The greedier ones always think that perhaps there is something nicer still in the bag too! So it can be very tedious during the feeding of a flock of sheep when a number of them continually try to push round immediately in front of you and stand in the way, often making it very difficult to move. The farmer can sometimes adopt the ruse of scattering a little food and then breaking away to fill troughs or spread feed elsewhere whilst most of the sheep are distracted. Feeding on the ground is easier when the person holding the bag can run just ahead of the flock emptying out a row of feed. Doing so into troughs it is a little more difficult to ensure that none spills; but if the ground is wet or muddy, then troughs are necessary. In wet or snowy weather these have to be emptied each morning before being filled with food. Hungry sheep jumping over and into the troughs do not facilitate this!

One of the compensations of having to go out daily in all weathers and all seasons, to feed or check beasts, is that there is always something of interest to see about the farm. At this time of year, even knowing that it is premature, we start to look for signs of the new year beginning, and one of the first of these is frog spawn. Sometimes, when I walk or drive past a puddle or pond, I notice a little movement in the water as a frog submerges, but mostly it is just a matter of noticing that frogspawn has appeared. Sometimes it can be seen in the first week of March, and it is always during the first half of the month. We can find frogspawn in even quite small puddles, often in silly places that are certain to dry up before the tadpoles hatch. Usually, within a few days, at some stage or another, we see these puddles frozen after a night's frost. This probably does not damage the spawn, but one always feels that the frogs are a little premature in their activities. Frogs seem to prefer shallow water for spawning, and if they do so in ponds it tends to be around the shallow edges, whereas toads will deposit their spawn in deeper water. Frogs lay spawn in a mass or lump, and if many frogs spawn in the same place the jelly-like spawn forms into a great accumulation. Toad spawn is deposited in strings, wound around underwater plants or submerged twigs and other obstacles. Judging by their attraction to small ponds and waterholes at this time of year, both mallard and herons may be partial to frogspawn.

Newts lay their single eggs a little later than frogs and toads, usually in April, and carefully attach these to pond weeds. We have palmate newts in our ponds, and see them in the water occasionally in spring. One spring we found one in our front porch, and that same year a neighbour twice had one come actually into his sitting room, presumably the newt having squeezed under the door! All three of these amphibians, though they appear very much at home in water actually spend most of the year, other than breeding time, on land. Newts are rarely seen on dry land, but come out at night to hunt for worms and slugs. They migrate to ponds in the early part of the year to breed in the same way as frogs and toads, and presumably those entering the house were moving around looking for a pond. Sometimes, if one looks carefully in the ponds in April one may see a newt tadpole swimming about. Unlike frog and toad tadpoles, newt tadpoles look like tiny mini-newts, although they have feathery external gills. They usually emerge later than frog tadpoles but I have seen them before any frog or toad tadpoles have hatched out. The young newts do not swarm in a mass like other tadpoles, since their eggs are laid individually on pond weed by the female newt. All of these tadpoles are cannibals and the larger ones will prey upon, and feed on, the smaller and weaker ones, and they will also eat carrion such as a dead fish or a rotting rabbit carcase in the water as a change from vegetable matter and algae.

One can distinguish frog and toad tadpoles by colour. Those of frogs are a sort of brownish colour with some lighter spots or flecks, whereas toad tadpoles are black. We have seen quite large tadpoles swimming about in the ponds in autumn. This is due to a prolonging of the larval state, known as neoteny. This

may be caused by cold water. It is apparently commoner in newts than in frogs; however it is frog tadpoles that we have generally noticed at pond edges not having metamorphosed. They may do so the following spring if they survive that long, but their chances of survival are slim. Sometimes in August we find little black toadlets hopping about.

Weary after the long winter, anxious about the food supply lasting out, and eagerly looking forward to the prospect of warmer longer days and new grass growth, we seek signs of the new year beginning and spring approaching. Anxiously we await the arrival of the nesting birds, the most prominent of which are the lapwings, the oystercatchers, the blackheaded gulls and the curlews. The former are sadly not as abundant as once they were, but we always have a few pairs in the fields, and usually half a dozen pairs on a flat field up on the hill. Usually we first hear and see a small flock of lapwings at the end of February, but sometimes they do not appear until March has begun. Often they stay only a few days at first, and disappear when there are snow showers and a bad spell of weather, to reappear later in the month. The oystercatchers, or red-nibs, and the blackheaded gulls arrive a few days later. We have recorded them in the last days of February, but generally it is the first week in March that they appear. Sometimes the first sign of the return of the oystercatchers is when they call overhead in the darkness, but other times we suddenly notice them and the gulls sitting in a field. The blackheaded gulls are not in full breeding plumage when they arrive, but soon change into their smart chocolate brown hoods and bright red beaks and legs. There were none when we first came to the farm, but gradually they colonized one of the ponds that we built, and then another, and then a third. The last one was not a success, and I suspect that a fox raided the nests and took the eggs, and the gulls did not return to it. Foolishly a few gulls had nested on the bank. On the other ponds they built nests in the reeds surrounded by water, which is safer. The blackheaded gulls seem to appear gradually, with their numbers increasing daily, and the colony assumes breeding plumage and becomes noisier as pairing takes place.

Oystercatchers appear in pairs on the farm. Perhaps the flocks broke up into breeding pairs earlier, further down the river, before splitting off to head up into their nesting territories in the fields. There is a certain amount of flying rapidly about overhead, twittering loudly as pairs vie for territory, but mostly they seem to settle for a pair occupying each field. They spend quite a lot of time standing around or preening, interspersed with bursts of feeding activity. When feeding they peck the ground repeatedly, sometimes at every pace or two, and at others hurrying several yards before pecking again. Much of the time it would seem that the pecks are exploratory, not yielding food, but why this is so seems uncertain. Maybe the pecks at the ground are at likely spots for containing worms that are not pursued if the ground is found to be hard, but which are investigated further if it is found to be a worm tunnel. Every now and again the oystercatcher will thrust its beak completely into the ground up to its nostrils and then clearly struggle to grasp something and then eventually draw out a worm like a piece of spaghetti and suck this up from the end of its bill.

Of all the birds though, it is the curlew for which I listen most eagerly in early March. I could not imagine spring without the sound of curlews filling the air, and could not bear to live without the noise of their calls in the early part of the year. Waking on a sunny morning in April to listen to the curlews calling on the hill is to me one of those magical sounds that produces a sense of excitement and well-being like hearing a much-loved, wonderful piece of music. The first curlews come singly, but after a few days they fly down to gather in a flock in the field behind the house in the evenings, sometimes twenty or thirty of them. Gradually, after a couple of weeks, they split into pairs for nesting on the hill and the flock dwindles. This seems to be a gradual process, with groups of curlews feeding in the fields at different times of day, and odd ones here and there, as gradually the numbers on the pastures decrease and more stay throughout the day on the hill. Once the territories are established the birds fly over them, gliding and hovering and giving their haunting and beautiful bubbling calls.

March weather is variable. We can have lovely, sunny, mild mornings, and we can also have cold driving winds with rain or snow, that are hard upon the cattle and sheep. March can come in 'like a lamb' and go out 'like a lion' all too often. Walking around the ewes on a sunny morning enjoying the sound of the curlews it is easy to forget that spring is still a long way off and bad weather is certain before the days start to get warmer. Ewes that are in bad condition, due to age, lack of teeth, illness or whatever, tend to fare badly as their lambs grow inside them, and they can become so weak that they have difficulty in righting themselves if they overbalance when lying in rough ground, because of the weight that they are carrying inside. Similarly a thick wet fleece can weigh down the ewe, and the shepherd has to be vigilant, as lambing approaches and the sheep grow heavy, for any that become 'couped', or turned over on their backs unable to rise. Sheep can die very quickly in such a predicament, the weight of their internal organs in the wrong position suffocating them. Sheep in poor condition lose their wool easily, especially when handled, and may lose some after lying on frozen ground or rubbing against fences or trees. This wool is appreciated by many birds for their nests. Jackdaws in particular like sheep's wool for lining their nests in holes.

These birds can be a considerable nuisance, and even danger as a result of their nesting habits, for they frequently regard chimneys as ideal nest holes, despite these seeming to us to be most unsuitable – I often wonder how the birds can flutter up chimneys to get out again. Sometimes they do not, and we have had a filthy black, exploratory jackdaw emerge into a room, to the consternation of us all, creating much mess before it was captured and released outside. Attempting

to clean a chimney one spring, in a room in which no fire had been lit for a while, I discovered a blockage, and I had to use a rod with hooks to drag debris down the chimney from what had been a jackdaw's nest. This consisted of a massive pile of twigs, and a quantity of sheep's wool, all of which filled two large sacks. The small dry twigs would have made fine kindling wood, and had a fire been lit in the hearth with the nest still in the chimney it is likely that a spark would have ignited a massive chimney fire, from which much of the smoke would have come back into the room as a result of the blocked chimney. Thereafter we have been careful to put wire over little-used chimney pots to prevent access by jackdaws. Those chimneys with constant fires prevent their access of course. We have even had a goosander sitting on our chimney pot . Working at my desk on farm papers early one morning I heard strange, rather guttural grunting noises and located these as coming down the chimney. I went outside to see a male goosander sitting on top of the chimney pot, perhaps prospecting for a nest too!

I have no evidence of jackdaws menacing lambs, as is the case with the other corvids, although I suspect their presence in the farmyard is not desirable if exposed bantam nests are present. Consequently I am not alarmed when I see them walking about on the backs of sheep, and even on their heads. The sheep do not seem to mind their familiarity, and probably realize that the jackdaws are relieving them of parasites such as ticks and lice. One would have thought that a couple of jackdaws hopping about on a ewe's back, and especially upon her neck and head, would be irritating, but the sheep appear to remain oblivious until presumably an extra strong peck causes the animal to shake its head; at which point the bird may flutter onto the animal's back or onto the ground close by, but does not seem alarmed or disconcerted. Magpies will also walk about or stand on sheep that are lying down, and are clearly tolerated, presumably in return for the removal of pests, but I am always concerned that an adventurous magpie might risk a peck at an eye, considering the rapidity with which they will descend on these in the case of dead sheep and lambs. This behaviour is rather more common later in the season, so it is not a question of the birds collecting wool for nesting material.

Nature has ways of applying 'safety valves', and one of these is the facility of a ewe to lose her lambs if the stress upon her body metabolism is too much. If sheep get in too low a condition earlier in the year they can sometimes resorb the embryos to save energy for themselves, or later in pregnancy they can abort the foetus. Abortions are often caused by disease and can cause considerable losses in a flock, but tests carried out upon a series of aborted foetuses have inevitably produced inconclusive results, with a high proportion attributed to causes unknown. In a sizeable flock of outwintered sheep an occasional abortion seems to be inevitable. With sheep running on the hill it is often difficult to know whether ewes that fail to have a lamb are barren, failed to conceive or be served in the first place, or whether they aborted the foetus at an early stage. Signs on the ewe, such as a little blood at her back end, are not always easy to spot, and foxes and crows soon clear up any evidence.

Abortions can be caused by a variety of diseases in sheep, and it is quite usual to expect up to 2 per cent of lambs to be lost thus. Even in well-tended flocks lamb losses from various causes of up to 15 per cent are normal during the period before lambing and within the first ten days of life, due also to stillbirths and death soon after parturition resulting from hypothermia or lack of milk from the ewe, and a host of infections to which new-born lambs are susceptible.

In the period before lambing is due to start the farmer has to be vigilant for any signs of unusual behaviour in the sheep, particularly if there is bad weather. Any ewes that seem to be abnormally slow, away on their own, or off their food, could be showing signs of illness. Sheep that are thin, due to hard winter weather, poor feed, or tooth wear and age, or to carrying a large lamb or twins, are vulnerable to the possibility of pregnancy toxaemia, also known as twin lamb disease. This is basically caused by the embryo lambs taking too much out of the system of an already weak ewe. Much the same conditions, often exacerbated by stress or excitement, or even movement to different fields, can result in hypocalcaemia and also hypomagnesaemia, which can be fatal. These problems are caused by shortage of calcium and magnesium in the body, which can be treated if

spotted in good time. Sheep off on their own, lying down and looking lethargic, sleepy or even semi-conscious, are likely to be suffering from these problems near lambing time.

March can be a month of worry and preparation for the hill farmer. Lambs provide a substantial part of his income, and disaster in the form of bad weather or disease can have a significant effect on the proceeds of the autumn lamb sales. Most people receive some regular form of income, be it a weekly wage or a monthly salary, but the hill farmer derives most of his income from the sales of lambs and calves in the autumn, together with any subsidy payments usually paid also in autumn or late winter, and there is often a long period in spring and summer with no money coming in. A poor lambing means long anticipation of probable poor sale proceeds.

We generally bring the ewes off the hill into a field beside the farm about two weeks before lambing is due, so that we can keep a better eye on them and look out for any problems, and to ensure that they have settled into the lambing fields with the change of environment well before the lambing starts. At this time we prepare the lambing pens, ready for housing any problem ewes or lambs. We erect these in an open-ended building, with plenty of air but out of the wind, and with the shelter of a good roof. A series of metal hurdles that lock together, with the floor well strawed, makes useful pens, and there is a tap in the building next door, fed by a pipe running to the old mill dam on the hill above, which gives a good supply of water, each pen requiring a bucketful when occupied.

March is recognized as the year's beginning by birds too, for the ducks, geese and turkeys start laying early in the month. Indeed the stag turkey starts displaying long before then, particularly on fine days. Few hill farmers keep poultry to any extent now, for the economics of doing so are doubtful. However many keep the odd hen or two that scratch around the yard and in the adjacent fields, being shut up only at night when they have gone to roost, to protect them from the ever-increasing number of foxes in the countryside. Unfortunately that alone is not sufficient protection because many foxes take poultry in broad daylight and often very close to the house. There can be little doubt that the fox having become not only suburban, but even urban, living in large cities, is creating a considerable problem. Not only does it appear that these urban foxes are inferior specimens, often in poor condition, but they represent a substantial breeding reservoir to spill out into the countryside. Whereas the country foxes are governed by food supply, particularly in hill areas where they may have large territories, the urban foxes may have a constant supply of food in the form of scraps from dustbins and litter and so on, although probably not such a healthy diet as their country cousins. Forced changes in agricultural practice, and thus the countryside, through set-aside policies and encouragement to plant small farm woodlands, coupled with the massive increase in the rabbit population, all result in the probability of a further increased fox population throughout the country.

Whereas the damage done by foxes in low country areas may be limited to problems with reared gamebirds, and in some cases to free-range piglets, in hill areas they represent a significant danger to lambs when other food sources are not abundant. Round the farmyard hens and ducks that lay out in bushes or on the burn bank, and sit on their eggs, are under threat from foxes, as well as from mink, which have spread alarmingly in some districts from a few original escaped animals, and are now firmly resident.

Because of very early daylight in the summer, and the early emergence of all poultry to go foraging soon after it is light, we do not shut the door on our geese and ducks in the long days. One morning in summer at 4 a.m. my wife heard the geese yelling and looked out of the window to see them running down the track in front of the house in panic. She hurried out and they spontaneously ran into their shed, and she shut the door on them. On her way back into the house she saw the sheep in the field in front of the house looking at something and realized that it was a fox standing there. Happily the geese were all safe, but a few days later we missed a duck and found the remains of one of the Aylesburys in the field, and a few days later another suffered the same fate, so we reverted to shutting them up at night, delaying their early morning foraging until a safer time.

The previous winter we lost our Aylesbury drake to an otter. There was a blizzard one evening, and intent on getting the hens safely into shelter we did not

notice that the drake was not in the house with the other ducks. In the morning when we discovered him missing I searched the banks of the burn, all covered in snow. Eventually I found him cowering under a bush, still alive, but with both breast muscles bitten almost off and a deep bite on his back; so I had to kill him. The otter tracks were plain to see in the snow, and in fact I followed these out of curiosity. They continued up the burn to the old mill dam and then a short way up the tiny burn feeding this, at which point the tracks turned and headed downstream again. Several years earlier we had put some trout into that dam, and for some months we fed them regularly. One day there was suddenly no sign of fish where a couple of days before they had greedily come for their feed. We examined repeatedly all the causes that could be imagined, such as netting by poachers, mink, herons, escaping down the burn, and so on. There were no clues visible and none of the explanations suggested by others seemed satisfactory. We had not thought of otters, for though we knew that they regularly travelled up the main burn in the valley below we never expected that they came up as far as the dam, following the small burn through the farmyard. The proof of this, clear tracks in the snow, resulted in the otters becoming a prime suspect.

The eggs laid by our truly free-range hens are often a source of surprise to those that only see shop-bought eggs normally, for even allegedly free-range eggs, that are sold as such, may have pale, insipid-looking yolks compared to the deep orange of the yolks of hens feeding on grass, insects and seeds in a completely natural way. Proper free-range hens are not curtailed in their wanderings by any fence at all, and generally follow the well-known country maxim of early to bed and early to rise. Although farmyard hens welcome a supplement of food in the form of wheat or barley, it is clear that they like a variety of diet and will only eat a certain quantity of offered food before going off to forage. When let out of their houses in the morning ducks and geese generally make straight for clean water for a bathe, if given the opportunity, and naturally-kept ducks in the farmyard spend most of their day on or near any stream or pond that is nearby. Most hill farms have water in or near the farmyard, because the houses were built near a water supply, and so ducks and geese kept on these farms generally have ideal natural conditions in which to live, unlike most of the ducks and geese reared commercially in large quantities for eating, which may never have access to plentiful clean water in which to swim and bathe. Ducks prefer feeding in water too, and go to barley thrown into the pond or burn rather than to that put onto dry land.

Our turkeys are not shut up at night since they roost on top of a gate or in the lower branches of a tree or on the roof of a shed, which they seem to prefer even in stormy weather. They could go to roost in a building or in the Dutch barn, but rarely enter a building and seem to prefer it outside. Perhaps because they are allegedly American wild turkeys with a possible touch of Norfolk Black blood they are happier outdoors. Although completely free to go where they choose they rarely stray far from the farmyard, and nest in the ivy on the stone dykes around the garden, or in clumps of nettles, laying quite well in early summer. Their eggs are excellent to eat, like double-sized hen eggs with small reddish-brown spots. The turkeys go to roost at dusk, usually after the other poultry, and leave their perches at dawn.

March is the arrival time for many birds, and the variety at our bird table is encouraged by a birch wood close by, as well as the various tall shrubs that we have planted in the garden, sheltered by trees. Siskins gradually appear in increased numbers at this time of year, and we notice their bright breeding plumage increase as the month progresses. The tits that were numerous, feeding on peanuts and bird seed and discarded fat, gradually become less frequent outside the window as more food becomes available for them elsewhere, and doubtless their thoughts turn to nesting, until gradually the charming little siskins seem to monopolize this food supply. As pairing begins to take place and territories become established cock chaffinches occasionally start to sing on fine days, and in the fields and on the hill, especially where beasts have been fed, pied wagtails suddenly appear. We see the yellow wagtails, that seem to prefer being near water such as burns or ditches, a little later in the year. One season a wagtail nested in the cab of an old tractor that stood unused for a time in summer, and I had to abandon ideas of using it until the fledglings left the nest. Another season, working nearby, I noticed a wren enter my tractor cab through a gap in the rear window, and later investigation revealed a nest hidden away in the roof of the cab in a corner wedged behind the sponge rubber lining. Again I had to forgo use of that tractor until the young had flown. Fortunately it was a time of year when tractor use was less vital and I had the old tractor as a substitute! The following year there was another nest in the opposite corner under the roof. Perhaps the same bird remembered the site, or maybe it was simply a wren's idea of the ideal spot for nesting and so an obvious place to choose for any wren.

In March we often see flocks of woodpigeons in the field outside our kitchen window. Since we grow no arable crops, having only a few fields for hay or grazing, these birds are not a pest to us as they are to farmers with cereals, oilseed rape or vegetable crops. At this time of year the sprouting young clover leaves are the attraction to the pigeons, and the flocks peck away at these until their crops are bulging. Many people only see woodpigeons flying in the distance, or dead, but when one has the opportunity to see and study them close up one can appreciate what beautiful birds they are, with superb colours of grey, blue, pink and white. They always appear such clean and tidy birds, though they can wreak havoc amongst seedlings in the garden at times.

By now ermines are changing or have already changed back to stoats, especially if there have been some fine warm days. That is to say that the white stoats are reverting to brown as they shed their winter coats and take on their sleeker summer ones. This is a more gradual process than the instant overnight change to white in the middle of winter when snow occurs, and often we see skewbald stoats, in partially changed colour condition, running about along the edges of fields or hunting along stone dykes or amongst gorse.

By the end of the month the hawthorns are showing a tinge of green and the buds of the gean trees are swelling. We generally pick a few gean, or wild cherry, twigs to put in a vase of water so that the blossom comes out early in the house before it does on the trees outside. Next month the blossom on the gean trees will rival any almond blossom in Portugal, and later on when the bird cherry is out the display is superb. Bird cherry has an extremely strong, sweet scent – almost too strong if we have a few sprigs in the house. The bird cherry is host plant, or tree, to a moth, whose name I can never remember, but I believe may be the small ermine moth. However, the caterpillars of this moth are spectacularly obvious, for they festoon the trees in summer with a cocoon of silk, often enshrouding the entire tree including the trunk right down to the ground beneath a tent or web of silk underneath which thousands of caterpillars consume every green leaf. The remarkable thing is that not only does this not kill the tree, but in late summer new leaves appear and the trees seem normal again. Occasionally one finds that if one picks twigs in April, for early blossom in the house, little webs of silk appear around some of the leaves emerging from opening buds, and inside these tents of web one can see a mass of tiny caterpillars at work. Both caterpillars and webs grow in size, until finally the web would cover the whole twig, though generally by then the flowers have faded and we put the foliage outside. The bird cherry berries later in the season are bitter and alas inedible.

The birch buds are filling out too and starting to show green and the little male catkins that have been on the twigs since the previous autumn begin to mature ready for the emergence of the female catkins. The swelling buds and the growing catkins are relished by browsing animals and readily eaten by cattle, sheep and ponies, and both red deer and roe deer will carefully nip these off the twigs, whereas the domestic animals tend to just bite off the whole end of the twig. I watched some red deer feeding on a branch of a birch tree that had broken off in the gales of early March, and later I went to see what they had been eating. Had I not seen them feeding on the branch I should never have noticed that it had been browsed, but close examination revealed all the little male catkins carefully nipped off the twigs. Deer like pungent bog myrtle too in the spring, and patches near our ponds are heavily browsed, with the tops of the plants more obviously eaten. The lovely spikes of crimson male flowers are borne on only a few of the bog myrtle plants, most carrying the fatter female buds. The bog myrtle flowers towards the end of March.

In the garden signs of colour slowly start to appear, and in sheltered spots the red dead-nettle starts to flower, and in the flower bed the little white bittercress flowers are evident on the small plants. These are really weeds, but then weeds are

only plants that are out of place! On warm, still, sunny days one can hear the buzz of bees and see some flying about, and occasionally a butterfly will flutter across the hill. However they have to be wary for the end of March seems invariably to bring the 'teuchat storms' or equinoctial gales. Some say that there is no evidence that the equinox, when the length of the day and night are equal, brings gales, but our experience is that it is most likely to do so. The vernal, or spring, equinox is on 21 March. This can be a bad time for early new lambs, for driving rain on a bitterly cold, easterly gale can be a killer causing hypothermia in lambs, and scour in calves.

April

April is a busy and exciting month on the farm. There starts to be a feeling of spring in the air on fine days. The fields begin to look a little greener, even if grass growth is still some way off . The first wood anemones, or windflowers, appear on the hill under the birches early in the month, and daily the mornings and evenings seem to grow noticeably longer.

The woodcock, which we first saw roding in March, now regularly makes his ritual croaking flight over the farm from the birch wood at dusk. The male bird tours his territorial area on an evening patrol flight each night, and generally we hear his croaking call before seeing him. The sparrowhawk must be familiar with the woodcock's routine too, for we find the feathers and remains of woodcock

around the farm from time to time. Sparrowhawks have increased in numbers considerably in the past few years, to the stage where they may be beginning to become a nuisance at bird feeding tables in gardens, and also in further reducing the numbers of small birds, such as yellowhammers, linnets and redpolls, and even the now scarce indigenous grey partridge. I suspect that they also take the lapwings, unfortunately, judging by remains found about the farm and on the hill from time to time. One summer a pair of white doves appeared in the farmyard and took up temporary residence, availing themselves of the grain put out for the hens in the mornings. Going around the corner of the farm buildings into the yard one day I spied something white upon the ground beside a door into a building, and at the same instant saw a grey object fly off at speed. I realized that the white object was one of the doves, which had been attacked by a sparrowhawk. Apart from missing a few feathers it seemed unharmed, and I saw it with its mate in the yard for the next day or two. Then one day only the male dove was present, and soon afterwards he too vanished. I presumed that the sparrowhawk had taken them. We see sparrowhawks flashing past the windows quite often, and hear the alarm calls of small birds and see them dashing into thick bushes for cover. The sparrowhawk is a prime suspect for the disappearance of small chicks from our farmyard.

For many years a kestrel roosted in our Dutch barn, a big open-sided shed used for storing hay bales. Kestrels are now quite a common sight in the countryside, perched on telephone wires or on the top of a small tree, or sometimes dining upon the remains of a rabbit carcase on the road. We often see them soaring and hovering over the hill, occasionally stooping for a vole or an insect on the ground. Merlins have become more common too and although these birds are really inhabitants of large areas of open moorland and hill ground, recently we have seen one around the farm, and one day a friend driving across our farmyard saw one flash past in front of the vehicle and snatch a small bird within a few yards of his windscreen and swoop off with it. Merlins are the smallest of the four falcons in this country. The other falcons are the hobby, which is a rare summer visitor to the southern parts of the country only, the kestrel and the peregrine. Falcons are distinguished from hawks by their shape, with more pointed wings, designed for speed and diving down, or stooping, on prey. Falcons also have a different-shaped beak, with a sort of notched beak or serration, like a kind of tooth, which they use for killing their victims by biting them, usually at the back of the head. Hawks tend to kill their struggling victims by squeezing them in powerful talons as they fly off with them, and then devour them when settled on a suitable place. We see many hawks from our windows too. Buzzards are now very common and we can see these from the house out of almost any window, and often several together. Occasionally we can see a hen harrier gliding across the fields, and we have glimpsed a goshawk.

Soon the ground in the birch woods is a carpet of wood anemones, and this is the time of year that the roe deer start to emerge from the shelter of the conifer plantations to take up residence for the summer in more open ground. The roe deer like wood anemones to eat, and the appearance of these, together with other new grown vegetation brings the deer out eager for fresh feed. Deer of all species seem to be very fond of flowers to eat, and later in the year I have watched roe deer plucking broom flowers from the bushes on the hill, and in late summer I have watched red deer hinds picking off the broom seed pods. The roe deer still have their thick winter coats, but the bucks are beginning to shed the velvet from their antlers. Some of the slender willow saplings round the edges of the woods, and young conifers in recently planted shelter belts, show signs where the roebucks have frayed to scrape the loose velvet from their antlers, and to start marking out new summer territories. The 'velvet' is the skin covering, rich in blood vessels, under which the bony antler growth occurs each year, until finally hormone development causes this blood supply to the antlers to be cut off and the skin covering shrivels and peels off, aided by the buck scraping the dried up remains on saplings. This scraping causes the white antlers to rapidly become stained brown from the tree sap, especially when conifers are the trees used for the purpose.

From 1 April we start to supplement the hay fed to the cows with cattle cobs containing magnesium, to counter any problems of magnesium deficiency which could lead to a condition known as hypomagnesaemia, or 'staggers', which can be fatal if not treated rapidly. This results from the rapid growth of herbage, particularly in artificially fertilized fields, where the uptake of minerals from the soil is not sufficient in the quantity of grass eaten to maintain the cow's blood magnesium level; unlike some minerals, a cow cannot store magnesium as a reserve for use if it runs short and so she requires a daily intake. As the grass growth becomes less lush later in spring, so the mineral content is restored to a more satisfactory level, and by the middle of May we can cease the magnesium-rich supplement. Cattle on natural, unfertilized herbage are less likely to develop 'staggers', but there is still a risk. None of our grazing land receives any artificial fertilizer and so the risk is low, but we prefer to be cautious. Indeed we have now ceased applying artificial fertilizer even to the hay crops, since the economics seem doubtful, with the extra volume of crop achieved by such application appearing to be insufficient to justify the cost of buying and spreading the fertilizer.

The spring calving starts in April, so that the cattle have to be watched for problems too, as well as the sheep. With hill cows of indigenous breeds, and crosses, calving usually presents few problems, but, as with all animals, these can occur. Calves can be presented incorrectly or be large and difficult for a cow , or especially for a heifer, at parturition, and occasionally assistance is required. On the hill this can be difficult, and sometimes even finding a missing cow is not easy in broken ground and scrub shelter. Although most farmers will count their cattle each day at feeding time to check that they are all present, often one knows instinctively if a beast is absent. A missing cow has to be searched for and found and checked. Newly-calved cows sometimes delay bringing their calf down to join the others at the feeding place, and they may leave their new-born offspring tucked under a bush on the hill for the first two or three days. Others just appear in the morning with a calf trotting beside them. A missing cow may indicate trouble. If a cow that has obviously calved appears on her own, a check has to be made to see if the calf is all right. Cows can be very secretive and reluctant to lead a person to their calf, and often will not go to it if they know that they are being watched, so sometimes it is necessary to observe the cow when she has finished feeding and perhaps stalk her to find out where she has hidden the calf, or return later in the day to search the hill for her. The farmer learns from experience places where cows are likely to calve in differing weather conditions, which helps to reduce the search to some extent.

Newly calved cows need to be approached with some caution even by those with whom they are familiar, for the first day or two the new mothers can be very possessive and protective and a cow is a strong animal. A neighbouring hill farmer was moving his cattle to a clean field a couple of years ago, which involved them crossing through a wet muddy gateway. One very young calf was reluctant to go through the mud, so he picked it up and carried it. However the calf let out a yell and the mother turned round and charged the farmer and knocked him down and continued to butt him. With the breath knocked out of him he decided to feign dead and she left him, whereon he managed to crawl through a fence and get to his tractor. He suffered a number of broken ribs and was badly bruised and unable to work for some time. His wife and other neighbours had to do the essential work until he recovered. He was fortunate to have some neighbours close enough to be able to help .

April is lambing month for most hill farmers. For the majority, sheep are the main enterprise and lambing is the critical period of the year, which determines the major part of the farm income. A good lambing can make the future more appealing, but a bad lambing can be a disaster. In years past wool was an important commodity and sheep were kept specifically for the wool crop. A flock of wethers – castrated male sheep – was kept specially for wool production, and in due course these wethers were sold for mutton at perhaps three or four years old. However, for a good many years now the wool price has been poor compared to other commodities and as a consequence sheep are no longer kept specifically for their wool. Flocks became entirely ewe flocks that produced lamb for meat as well as wool, and mutton disappeared from the market altogether. The lamb for meat is much more important now than wool production, of which there is presently a world surplus. Consequently a successful lambing with a large number of lambs reared to weaning age determines a significant part of the hill farmer's livelihood, and this is dependent upon the level of lamb prices at sale time in the autumn. This may now be changing to some degree however, with the introduction of ewe quotas determining effectively how many sheep a farmer is allowed to carry on his farm, with subsidies paid on those ewes and not on lambs. In some places where sheep are very heavily stocked in hill country there can be little doubt that their constant browsing inhibits the regeneration of natural tree seedlings, and may have an adverse effect on heather and some areas of hill vegetation, but heavy overstocking acts adversely upon the sheep themselves in the reduction in food supply and increase in parasites and disease. On the other hand there are many areas where sheep are definitely beneficial to the environment and the natural flora, and this can be seen in some nature reserves where small flocks of sheep are deliberately brought in to keep down the grass and herbage to allow the shorter-growing plants to thrive. The same applies to many areas of hill ground, which would quickly revert to birch scrub without the sheep to check this. Many of those that preach a requirement to allow natural tree regeneration to proliferate do not appreciate that large areas of thick birch growth or willow scrub are neither beneficial nor attractive. Birch thickets, for instance, grow into areas of thin spindly birch trees with such a close canopy that nothing grows beneath them for many years, and such regeneration does not necessarily become the attractive open birch woodland that so many seem to imagine. Examples of this can be seen on many roadsides.

The fortnight or so before lambing commences always seems to bring the start of any problems, such as abortions, couped sheep and weak ewes finding the stress too much. Unfortunately weaker ewes tend to be bullied at the feeding places as the strong sheep push them out of the way to grab food first, so their disadvantage increases. Hungry ewes are not gentle animals. Wet weather can also causes fleeces to become heavy and increases the danger of ewes well advanced in lamb becoming couped, or falling onto their backs, when lying in some sheltered place or uneven ground, rendering them unable to rise. Bringing sheep off the hill onto more level ground before lambing enables a closer watch to be kept on these problems. Ditches and narrow burns are a danger for ewes heavy in lamb, for sometimes they go for a drink but because of the heavy weight of lambs that they are carrying, especially if they are not in very good condition after hard weather, they may have difficulty in getting out again and overbalance and coup. If they fall into the water the shock and cold will kill them. During the past winter we had trouble with dogs from three distant neighbours hunting rabbits on our hill. The dogs appeared in three different pair combinations on a number of occasions, with a spaniel and whippet combination being the most frequent. Several times I discovered the dogs in the same area as the in-lamb ewes, despite reporting this to the owners. Although I never saw the dogs bothering the sheep I did find ewes lying dead in ditches twice, and these could easily have been panicked into falling into the water just by seeing the strange dogs or hearing the spaniel yapping. Fortunately the spaniel has now moved from the vicinity!

Having applied paint or heavy wax crayon to the chest of tups in early November, when they were introduced to the ewes, the shepherd will have a close idea of due lambing dates by observing the dates on which the backsides of ewes became marked. As with all animals, the precise theoretical dates of gestation do not always apply, though they give a good general guide. Ewes can lamb up to at least a fortnight either side of due dates on occasions. Moreover, unless the farmer changes the colour of the paint on the tups it may be difficult to determine which ewes were tupped twice, having failed to conceive on the first tupping and being retupped three weeks later in the cycle. The average gestation period for a ewe is 147–150 days; for a cow it is 283 days.

Most farmers try to ensure a reasonably short lambing period rather than a long drawn-out one with a considerable variation of ages, and thus sizes, of lambs in a flock. This is achieved by trying to ensure that ewes come into season and conceive within the first three-week cycle after the introduction of the tups, and certainly within the first two cycles, giving a maximum lambing period of six weeks. Like deer, both male and female sheep come into season in the autumn, and unlike cattle that can come into season and breed all year round. Some hill breeds of sheep tend to come into season later than low ground breeds. So, to some extent, lambing dates are fixed within a period by nature. Some low ground farmers practise early lambing or even lambing three times in two years, but this is achieved by using the few breeds of sheep that either can come into season early and so lamb early, or an unusual breed, such as the Dorset Horn, that is capable of breeding at other periods of the year. Putting tups, or rams, into ewes early is unlikely to alter the breeding pattern except to result in a more straggly lambing period, and later in the breeding cycle ewes may tend to shed fewer eggs and so be less likely to produce other than single lambs. The major factor is the condition of the sheep, both ewes and tups, at mating time. This does not mean having them all in fat condition, but rather in good, and especially rising, condition, and it is a usual practice to put ewes on to good grazing a week or two before tupping to 'flush' them into rising condition, to give better prospects for good conception.

The use of an optimum number of tups is also important, for with too few, especially if the ewes are grazing on a large area, a ewe in season might be missed at the critical time for conception whilst the tup or tups are paying attention to another ewe elsewhere. Too many tups may simply result in fighting and squabbling over ewes and interfere with mating. Whilst a strong tup may be able to serve substantially more ewes, and a tup lamb may cope with less, about thirty to forty ewes per tup is a rough guide. However much depends on the circumstances, and upon the conditions prevailing, and the type and ages of the sheep involved, and farmers will undoubtedly have their own ideas. Where lambs are bred for sale for slaughter, rather than for breeding purposes, a ram or tup of a differing breed from that of the ewe is often used, partly to perhaps produce better confirmation in the lamb than that shown by hill breeds of sheep, but also to benefit from the advantage of hybrid vigour in the offspring. The progeny from a first cross, as well as benefiting from the characteristics of both parents to some extent, mostly show faster growth rates and greater hardiness. This hybrid vigour shows a further smaller increase with a second cross but then loses its momentum with further crossses. For this reason lambs raised for slaughter, as opposed to breeding replacements, are often produced by mating a cross ewe such as a Mule (Swaledale crossed with Bluefaced Leicester) or a Greyface (Blackface crossed with Border Leicester) with a tup of Downland breed, such as a Suffolk, to give a fast-growing lamb with early fattening capability and good confirmation.

The hill farmer with some in-by grazing fields can produce a few of these cross lambs, but those without such better quality grassland and who have to rely on hardy sheep able to thrive on poor grazing cannot rear lambs of this type. So these latter farmers may be restricted to breeding pure hill lambs; some of the ewe lambs can be retained for breeding and some be sold as stock for cross breeding, while others and the wether lambs, are sold to lowland farmers for fattening on better land. Lambs from the hardy hill breeds are smaller and may grow more slowly than their cross-bred or lowground counterparts and consequently fetch less money when sold, particularly the wether (castrated male) lambs that can be used only for meat.

The first few hours of a lamb's life, like those of any other young creature, are vital. The hill farmer has to be vigilant for problems at lambing time, because weakly lambs that would otherwise die can sometimes be assisted to survive. Weak lambs, especially those from multiple births, where the ewe may be busy giving birth to, or attending, other offspring, can be in danger from predators. Of these probably carrion crows are the most troublesome, but rooks and magpies can be as much danger to lambs in some areas, and in wild country with a less abundant food supply foxes probably take a lot of young lambs. We generally see evidence of foxes in the lambing fields, no doubt searching for any afterbirths that have not been cleared away and inadvertently left lying. Occasionally known weak or small lambs disappear inexplicably, but one cannot apportion blame without evidence. One season a fox accounted for seventeen of our lambs killed in four nights, and perhaps more that disappeared before being recorded, but this was the work of an animal with a broken canine tooth and presumably in pain. The carcases mostly had just their soft stomach contents eaten after the lambs had been killed by their heads being crushed. A bullet put an end to the fox and the killing eventually, after a long nocturnal vigil to catch and deal with the culprit.

Corvids frequent the lambing fields and are an ever present danger to young lambs, since all these birds will endeavour to peck their eyes, and have been found to do so to lambs that are not dead but either too weak to move, or even sound asleep. The speed with which these birds locate and descend upon dead or sickly lambs is astonishing, and one can find pitiful newborn corpses still warm, with their eyes pecked out, even at first light when one would not imagine that the crows and rooks could see too far. I have shot a rabbit in the field in front of the

house from my bedroom window on several occasions as I got dressed, and by the time that I have quickly finished dressing and hurried out to fetch it the rooks have already been at it, or any seagulls that happen to be in the area, since herring gulls, and of course the far larger blackbacked gulls, take precedence over the corvids as they are larger and stronger. On two occasions we have found perfectly strong and well-grown lambs with an eye missing. Dead lambs invariably have eyes pecked out within a short time of their demise, and some probably before this. At this time of the year, with nesting taking place, the birds are hungry for an increased requirement of protein.

In addition to trying to safeguard the flock from predators at this critical time, the shepherd has to try to ensure that young lambs get onto their feet and have a drink of their mother's colostrum within a couple of hours of birth. Unfortunately mastitis is an ever present problem and sometimes a ewe will be infected in one half of her udder, which will mean insufficient milk if she has twins. Young lambs tend to lay claim to their own teat rather than to share, with the result that if anything is wrong with one teat or one side of the ewe's udder the lamb on that side will obtain insufficient or no milk, and will either get progressively weaker or die whilst its sibling thrives. When this occurs the shepherd has to be on the watch for a ewe with a single lamb and plenty of milk and two good teats, or one that has lost her lamb and has milk but no offspring of her own to suckle, and then persuade her to foster the weak lamb. Similarly a ewe may well not produce enough milk to feed triplets adequately and removing one of these to be fostered by another ewe may benefit them all. Fostering can be a tiresome and time-consuming job, but in recent years special pens have been developed to facilitate the procedure. Acceptance of a foster lamb depends upon the ewe recognizing the lamb by both smell and sound. The former is dependent not merely on contact or close proximity, but on the consumption of that ewe's milk, and this ultimately passing through the lamb. Sheep appear to be able to recognize their own milk products. Whilst some ewes may take readily to a foster lamb to relieve the pressure of milk in their udder, usually it takes about a week for acceptance, and sometimes even ten days, before it is safe to release the ewe from the adopter pen.

This special pen consists primarily of a stock in which the ewe is secured by the neck. This is a narrow gap in which the sheep can move its head up and down, but with a bar across it at the top to prevent her from lifting her head out of the slot altogether. She will have access to buckets containing water and food in front and can stand up or lie down as she wishes. Generally bars either side of the ewe prevent too much sideways movement, but enable a lamb to suck her from the side. A small pen surrounds this, and a lamb or lambs to be fostered are placed in this, so that they can suckle the ewe without her being able to move around or butt them out of the way. Thus the shepherd does not have to be on hand to protect the lamb each time it wants a drink, which saves him much time at a

period when he may have a number of such fostering ewes, as well as orphan lambs, to look after.

In recent years research has shown that one of the principal causes of death in young lambs is hypothermia. Although this may be precipitated by bad weather, or exacerbated by it, the prime cause is lack of internal heating and fuel, or in other words lack of food in the form of colostrum or milk. A very young lamb will only survive a few hours without suckling successfully, and if it does not do so it will rapidly lose body heat and then die. For years it has been traditional to warm weakly lambs by the farmer's stove, or even in a warm oven, but these days modern methods have replaced this system. The normal temperature of a lamb is 39°C. If the temperature registers below this it is chilled and requires both warmth and feed, either colostrum or milk depending upon its age. If the temperature is below 37°C the lamb is severely chilled and its body metabolism will not operate properly for the absorption of milk, and so the animal has to be warmed rapidly to above this level. This can be achieved efficiently by a blast of warm air all round it, using a fan heater in a closed but ventilated warming box blowing hot air onto and round a lamb lying on a grid of wire or weldmesh where the warm draught can circulate. The warm air both heats and dries the lamb. Cold rain can quickly reduce the body temperature of a weak lamb and rapid drying in warm air obviates heat loss by evaporation that occurs in the field. Once the temperature of the lamb has been increased above 37°C it is given a feed of colostrum, if within its first 48 hours or so, or milk thereafter. This may have to be given by stomach tube, since in that weak state the lamb is unlikely to be able to suck sufficiently well to absorb a proper feed.

Obviously the warming box has to be near a source of electricity, and the adopter pen and other lambing pens are generally in the shelter of a building, so this means that any sick lambs have to be carried back there by the farmer. Moving a ewe with sickly lamb or lambs can be a time consuming and frustrating business upon occasions, necessitating carrying the lambs a few yards and then putting them on the ground again, with the shepherd sometimes having to make lamb bleating noises to encourage the ewe, and then waiting for her to come to them, before proceeding a little further. If she loses contact with the lamb or becomes alarmed she may well run back to their original position and the procedure has to be started again.

During lambing time the farmer has to be on the constant lookout not only for births that are presenting problems, in order to help the ewe if necessary, but also for weak lambs that are not getting enough milk, or are too weak to suck from their mother to obtain the necessary fuel for the metabolism of their bodies and thereby suffer from hypothermia, or that may have wandered too far from a ewe preoccupied with other lambs, and so on. The farmer may also decide to mark lambs, so that he can identify them later and associate them with their mother or sibling, if there are a lot in the lambing field. He may also choose to castrate and tail the lambs using rubber rings, which has to be done as early as possible in the life of the lamb, and preferably on the first day soon after the little animal has dried and suckled and is looking reasonably strong. The procedure is very quick and rarely appears to cause the lamb much discomfort, and if so, then not for long. The tight rubber ring, applied with a special expanding tool, cuts off the blood supply to the tail or scrotum and causes this eventually to atrophy and slough off after perhaps a couple of weeks or more. In a few hill breeds of sheep the tail may be left on the animal as protection in harsh winter weather, but in the majority of sheep this is docked for the later benefit of the lamb or ewe itself. At various stages, if lush spring feeding is available, or if the lamb contracts internal worms, to which most sheep flocks are susceptible, the backside of the lamb or ewe can become messy. This attracts the attention of flies, which lay eggs on the mucky wool, and these soon hatch into maggots, which burrow into the warm, moist wool and start to feed on the flesh of the unfortunate sheep. Consequently it is important for the wellbeing of the sheep to keep their backsides as clean as possible, both by ensuring that where necessary the sheep are properly wormed, and that there is not excess wool to become fouled. On high ground with poor feeding this is less of a problem, and long tails may give added protection from bad weather, but where the farmer tries to ensure good feeding for lambs to grow well, removal of tails helps to reduce the risk of later maggot infestation.

In some low ground situations lambs can grow sufficiently rapidly to be sold for slaughter before male characteristics start to affect the carcase. In those cases

castration may be unimportant or unnecessary. Towards the middle and end of summer male lambs begin to show definite male characteristics with increased growth of testicles, prominent horn growth in horned varieties, and facial differences. Not only does the diversion of growth into such characteristics adversely affect fleshing quality, but ram (tup) meat becomes more strongly coloured and flavoured and is unsaleable. Moreover by autumn the tup lambs are beginning to show interest in the females, and this can affect the growth of both. Uncastrated tup lambs can become a definite nuisance by late autumn, as well as having little market value – other than the few that may be retained specifically to become breeding tups – with the result that for flocks unable to sell off all their lamb crop by, perhaps, early August, castration of males, to become wethers, is essential, and this applies to all hill farms, which are unable to finish lambs early in the season.

To the passer-by, peering over the dyke into the lambing field, the new lambs are a happy sight. Young lambs racing in a bunch up and down a bank, or running to their mother for a suckle, are a pleasing scene, as indeed are most young things. But the onlooker does not see the pit behind the steading with the disasters and losses suffered by the farmer. Some losses are inevitable, for lambs succumb in numerous ways, and especially after a night of unpleasant weather,

the farmer from time to time on his early morning round will find a lamb lying dead, often with no ewe near it, and with no indication of the cause. It might have been a breech birth during the night, or the lamb may have been dead already inside the ewe for some reason, or it may have been born on a cold wet night and died of exposure, particularly if the ewe had wandered off a little way to deliver another lamb. Whatever the reason, there are always dead lambs, and the farmer has the sadness, as well as the financial loss.

The lambs are but one of the manifestations of the new season however, and towards the middle of April the birch trees start to show green as the buds emerge. Here and there primroses begin to appear on the hill, flowers that are long past further south in low country. The frog spawn has hatched by mid-April and the edges of the ponds are swarming with tadpoles. The grass in the fields is showing green, and in sheltered damp places, and along the road verges, early grasses such as cocksfoot are starting to grow, but it is not until well into May in most years, that the grass in the fields grows sufficiently strongly to provide unsupplemented grazing for cattle and sheep. The growing season in hill country is short, six months at the most, and really only five months in normal years.

One swallow does not make a summer is the saying. We always look and listen eagerly for our first swallow to return. In an early season he – for the male (with the longer tail feathers) usually arrives back first – arrives at the end of April. Often we feel that he may regret arriving so early, when the weather is still cold and inhospitable. Nevertheless the cheerful twittering of the swallow sitting on the electricity wires across the farmyard is a joyful sound and a pleasant, eagerly awaited, reminder that warmer days of plentiful grass for the beasts will soon be with us for a while.

For the hill farmer the end of April is a time full of hope for the coming summer. Lambing is almost finished by the end of the month, and most of the worrying time is past. The grass in the fields and on the hill is starting to grow, and the farmers on better ground are busy cultivating their fields and sowing their remaining spring crops. On farms with cattle wintered inside these are being let out into the fields, fresh air and, hopefully, sunshine. Wild flowers are starting to appear in profusion on the hill in sheltered places, and birds are beginning to build their nests and to lay their eggs, and a few early ones have already done so. The cry of the curlew is heard constantly now in the hills and on the moors, intermingled with that of the oystercatchers in the fields as they fly rapidly over their chosen nesting territories calling loudly and twittering to their mates and rivals. May, and the beginning of summer, is just around the corner, and any day now the call of the cuckoo will start to be heard constantly.

The cuckoo is an amazing bird in many ways. Its range of habitat extends almost throughout the entire variety in this country, for it is not merely a bird of the hedgerows and woods, but also of open hill country. Indeed the meadow pipit, that nests on the ground in heather or grass tufts and so on, is one of the principal targets of its parasitic breeding habits, although throughout the country they will lay their eggs in the nests of a wide range of victim species. The marvel of cuckoos is not only their ability to mimic the egg colouring of their unwilling host's clutch, but their ability to time their laying so that it takes place just before the hen bird starts to sit. Although the colouring of the cuckoo's egg closely matches that of the others already in the nest, it is usually slightly larger, hardly surprising considering that the cuckoo is a far larger bird than most of its unfortunate victims. Without considerable research, which would involve the marking of cuckoos and their study over a period of years to give more certain answers, it is difficult to be sure, but it is presumed that some cuckoos specialize in laying their eggs in the nests of a particular species, for which their egg coloration is suitably adapted. Why or how some cuckoos specialize in one species or another is a mystery, though presumably those cuckoos that habitually spend their summer breeding season in open moorland country would be likely to specialize in laying in the nests of such birds as meadow pipits, whereas those that frequent the gardens in the south each year are

more likely to parasitize different species. The cuckoo generally lays its egg in the nest of its victim as she has finished laying her clutch and is about to sit, and somehow it times this so that the egg hatches about the same time as, or just before the rightful ones of the host bird. The young cuckoo is thus able to get off to a good start, and then shoves out any as yet unhatched eggs and its unfortunate nest mates to fall outside the nest and die whilst it attracts the attention of its feeding foster parents with its ever-gaping craw.

May

The notion that farming is a way of life rather than a job has much truth in it, for stock farming, like any occupation involving looking after animals, is full time; that means seven days a week. Animals do not recognize holidays, and they have to be fed or looked after regularly. When they are ill, or giving birth, they need regular attendance, and they need to be checked at least daily even when such conditions do not apply. Any animals showing abnormal behaviour in any way need to be carefully watched to establish the reason. Cattle or sheep showing a tendency to be on their own, or lying down when all the others are feeding, and especially if reluctant to rise on being approached, may indicate that they are unwell. Calves walking more slowly than normal, or especially with their ears held horizontally or lower, rather than upright and alert, are showing likely signs of illness or discomfort.

Lush new grass grows rapidly early in May, and the cattle turned into grazing fields have to be watched, particularly with regard to their movements. At this time of year the farmer with cattle has to be vigilant for 'staggers', caused by a deficiency of magnesium in the blood, in turn caused by a comparative deficiency of this mineral in the fast-growing herbage eaten. Feeding cattle cobs containing a high magnesium content helps to avoid this problem, but is no guarantee, for one cannot be sure that all cattle eating the cobs get the optimum intake, and occasional beasts are reluctant to eat the cobs at all. Stumbling or tripping might well be symptomatic, and the farmer failing to notice this, or ignoring it, could find that next day the cow is down and in spasms, or even dead, for staggers causes rapid death if untreated. If the symptoms appear, a large subcutaneous injection of a magnesium solution can have a dramatic beneficial effect if timely. A whole 400ml bottle of liquid may have to be injected, by means of a flutter valve, which controls the flow in a slow trickle. This problem is less likely to occur in permanent grass fields with a good content of clover and other broad-leaved plants, or on hill grazing, for these forbs tend to have a higher mineral content than grasses, and particularly more than grass forced by high applications of artificial fertilizer. On some farms staggers seems to be regarded as a fairly regular hazard, but proper provision of magnesium in cattle feed at the critical spring and autumn periods of the year should help to make occurrence rare.

Most hill cows are of hardy breeds, or cross-bred, and not expected to raise more than one calf or provide more milk than is needed. However some dairy crosses can produce a lot of milk, and these have to be watched at calving time, for the sudden demand upon the cow's body when the milk supply starts can divert minerals from the bloodstream, and in particular calcium. This can cause hypocalcaemia or milk fever, and cows that look to have particularly swollen udders or are displaying signs of distress may be showing symptoms, which can lead to the cow becoming comatosed, and eventually dying if untreated. The treatment for this is again a large injection subcutaneously, but this time of a calcium solution, delivered slowly. Milk fever weakens the heart and too rapid an injection of calcium can over-stimulate it and kill the cow. We had a Jersey cow for many years, which supplied us with milk for the house as well as rearing both her own and a bought-in calf. For years she was fine and calved with no trouble, but when she was ten years old she suddenly developed milk fever after calving and we had to call the vet. In future years we knew the form and gave her the injection automatically, before she developed problems. There is a method of injecting beforehand as a precaution if one knows the precise calving date, since this injection is given a few days before parturition. We tried this one year and all was well, but it was quite expensive and we thereafter reverted to the well-tried calcium injection after calving, because establishing the exact date of calving was not easy when the cow ran freely with the bull for some weeks, and often seemed to come into season again and attract the bull after the date that subsequently we realized the proper service had taken place.

The farmer standing leaning on the gate watching his cows may not simply be idle and enjoying the view, though the sight of cows happily grazing adequate grass after the long winter is a pleasing one. Most likely he is observing the animals closely to check that all is well and that all the animals appear to be normal. Much can be learned about the condition and wellbeing of animals by quiet observation, noting any abnormal symptoms or behaviour, however slight. All animals have their own characteristics and idiosyncrasies. Some cows and sheep are naturally quite tame and do not mind being handled, whereas others are neurotic and skittish. Some animals are always the first to come when called, others are very reluctant to come, or nervous. Some cows or young cattle will not eat magnesium cobs, and some like to stand a little way off on their own rather than with the group. Some sheep will not eat food provided in winter unless desperate. Some cows in the herd are clearly at the bottom of the 'pecking order' and bullied by the others, whilst others are obviously dominant. Getting to know these characteristics is an important part of stockmanship.

The cattle gradually wean themselves from winter feed once the grass is growing in abundance, and they start to pay little attention to, or ignore hay that is provided, and lose enthusiasm for gobbling up cattle cobs. This provided feed can be reduced in accordance with demand until it can cease altogether. We generally provide cattle cobs containing a high magnesium content until the somewhat arbitrary date of 18 May. One year I decided to save money and cease feeding cobs a fortnight earlier; but I detected early symptoms of staggers in a cow a couple of days later and had to get her into a building for injection, and I resumed feeding the others their dose of magnesium. Since this experience I have not ceased feeding high magnesium cobs earlier than this date.

For a single-handed hill farmer with cattle running outside on the hill, or even when they are brought down to spend part of the summer in fields, handling cattle is a major operation, and a traumatic one for the animals too. It is now required that all animals have eartags by which they can be identified. On many farms with plenty of labour, or where cows are calved inside buildings, or young cattle are in-wintered, this may present little problem. On a hill farm where calves are born outside, and may not be handled at all until several months old,

eartagging involves much planning and work especially when this has to be carried out by a farmer working on his own. Like so many of these schemes thought up and implemented by bureaucrats it is doubtful if any of them have ever undertaken such a job themselves, or indeed have any conception of the difficulties involved, let alone the problem of trying to read the number on a small eartag on a frightened bullock. Large ear tags have a propensity for catching in a fence or on undergrowth and getting torn out. Thus easily read large eartags are fine in theory on an ideal farm but can be less suitable in practice on a hill farm.

With the cattle back into the summer grazing fields or lower parts of the hill, and the grass growing well, it is a relief to be able to cease the daily carting of feed that has been a job for the past five or six months. Now that the hill is starting to show green with the growth of new grass, the ewes with their lambs can be put back onto their summer grazing. However, before doing this, they have to be dosed for worms and liver fluke, and possibly treated with an insecticide to protect them from ticks too. This involves gathering all the sheep into the pens, and then sorting the lambs from the ewes to avoid them all being in the race together for dosing, when there could be a danger of the large ewes crushing lambs. Moreover the adult sheep receive different doses from the lambs, and so it is simpler to administer these separately. A good sheepdog can assist a single-handed shepherd considerably in the pens, by moving sheep up into the race where the shepherd is working, as others that have been dosed are released. Once dosed the sheep can be put out on the hill to remain there until clipping time, with the shepherd walking round them to check them as best he can, keeping an eye out for problems or sheep that seem ill at ease. Generally sheep grazing out on the hill are less prone to flystrike and maggot infestation than those feeding on lusher ground, but it can still occur when they have dirty, long fleeces. As a matter of principle I regard with disfavour the dosing of sheep, or other animals, with chemicals or drugs unless the necessity is obvious, not only from the point of view of adverse side effects upon the sheep, or the high cost of the drugs involved, but also because of the concern about the possible effect upon those administering the chemicals.

May is the time of year when early purple orchids appear in the places where they are to be found regularly each year. The primroses are fading now, and dark blue patches of bugle are taking their place. Like so many wild plants, bugle was once used medicinally as a mild narcotic in ancient times, as was the somewhat similar looking plant selfheal, that flowers a little later in the summer, and was thought to assist the healing of wounds and alleviate sore throats. The banks and the sides of tracks and roadways are now showing plentiful colour from the spring wildflowers, though areas grazed by sheep tend to be bare of these, for sheep have a predilection for eating flowers. In places with heavy stocking of sheep, or in those with a high rabbit population, the attraction of both these animals for eating flowers and flower buds, and also young seedlings, has a deleterious effect upon the regeneration and proliferation of wildflowers. In the case of sheep, their eating of highly nutritious young growth might be excusable so far as some farmers are concerned, but rabbits can be utterly destructive in merely biting off flowers and buds and leaving them lying uneaten upon the ground. It is not uncommon to find whole patches of early purple orchids and other flowers with all the flowerheads bitten off by rabbits and lying wilting, destroyed apparently without purpose. The destruction of the flowerheads prevents seeding and the consequent spread, or even natural replacement of the flowering plants.

In the ponds the shallow edges are now swarming with multitudes of tadpoles, and a careful look can reveal newts on the bottom amongst the weeds, where they too have gone to breed. In some parts of the country where pollution is a problem these amphibians are becoming rarer, but in many hill areas they are still abundant, as are dragonflies and damselflies and other inhabitants of the pond and wet area environment. On the warmer May evenings bats can be seen flitting round the farm buildings and nearby. We have both Long-eared bats and Pipistrelles around our farm buildings. Although the former are larger, identifying the bats in flight, unless one is expert, is extremely difficult since both are very small animals and the size differential is not very great. We discovered a Long-eared bat flying about rather weakly in the middle of a sunny summer's afternoon, eventually landing on the ground. Fearful that it might be spotted by a cat we caught it and placed it on the wall of a building in the shade. When seen close up one can appreciate just how small bats are, since their large wingspan tends to give a deceptive impression of size. We found a dead Long-eared bat lying in a farm building one day, which gave a good opportunity for examination. On another occasion we found a Pipistrelle crawling up a shed wall, rather too exposed to the risk of being reached by the cat, which is fascinated by small moving objects, including blowing leaves which it chases in the yard. This was put safely out of reach. When one handles the tiny creature one realizes how they can squeeze into very small spaces to get into lofts and so on for daytime roosting.

We were rather excited to discover one night that we also have Natterer's bats on the farm, as these are rarer. We had been out looking at newts in one of the ponds that we have made, using a spotlight after dark. This is a good way to observe aquatic creatures, when it is a fine, still night and visibility in the water is good. A number of creatures, such as newts, come into shallower water at the edge of the pond at night. This particular pond is long and narrow, and though it dries up in summer it is full of palmate newts breeding at this time of year, and doubtless feeding on hatching tadpoles too. It also contains fascinating water beetles such as great diving beetles and silver beetles. While looking at these we were aware of several bats patrolling just above the water's surface a few yards in front of us. They were quite large bats with a slower wingbeat than some, but

most noticeable was the paleness of their bodies, contrasting with their dark wings, as they flew away from us.

At this time of year the roe deer are eager for the newly-grown herbage, and they can often been seen at the edges of fields or out on the hill in the mornings or evenings, or even during the day in quiet undisturbed areas where there is cover nearby in which they can shelter, and from which they emerge to feed. They are still in their winter coats and will show little sign of changing from the brownish grey to the summer coats of bright gingerish red until the end of the month. The roe are now establishing their summer territories in more open ground, where feeding is better, after sheltering in warmer conifer plantations, other woods and thick cover during the colder winter weather. In areas where the deer live the farmer will often see them as he goes about the farm, and where they are unmolested they become accustomed to his familiar movements and the noise of the tractor and are not especially alarmed. Open birch woods are favoured by roe deer in hill country, offering shelter as well as plenty of plants for feeding upon in between the trees, but some roe spend the summer high out on the hills, or even live there permanently, in heather, or frequenting small patches of bracken or other cover. Roe can even be found sometimes high up in open hill country in some areas where there is a little cover of long heather or rocky gullies, and have been seen over the 750m contour in winter.

The birches are fully out by now. A close look at birch twigs will show the little female catkin standing upright amidst the leaves, whilst the open and much larger male catkins dangle nearby. Often one can see evidence of pollen produced by trees as a yellow film on top of puddles of water, but occasionally one can see the pollen blowing off the trees, and this can be spectacular. I have often seen pollen blowing from pine trees, and I recall one day some years ago watching a huge cloud of it blowing from a stand of mature Scots pine trees below me. On another occasion I saw a cloud of pollen blowing from a field of rye. However, the most spectacular release of pollen that I have seen occurred quite recently. I was outside the house at midday on 1 May, listening to a cuckoo. We had had two very warm sunny days, and the birches on the hill were all in leaf. Suddenly there was a squall of wind and I looked at the hill, with the rushing noise of the wind through the trees, and I saw a great cloud of pollen blow off a tree. As I watched the whole hillside, which is covered in scattered birches over its lower half, suddenly let loose a vast cloud of pollen, which blew in a huge rolling mist. The whole of the top half of the hill became completely obscured by a green fog, giving quite an eerie sensation, for several minutes. I stared in amazement, incredulous that the trees could produce so much pollen. Had I not witnessed the first pollen erupting from the trees I might well have wondered with alarm what had caused the weird green cloud to envelope the hill. Birch trees are deeper rooted than some of the other indigenous trees of hill country and are believed to bring up minerals in their root systems and increase the fertility of the top layers of soil when these are passed into leaves that are subsequently shed onto the ground in autumn.

The other tree that is beneficial in a similar way, but which comes into leaf rather later, is the alder. This is the only tree in this country with nodules on its root system that are capable of fixing nitrogen from the air into the soil and increasing fertility. Thus the herbage in the vicinity of alder trees is often noticeably lusher as a result of the higher nitrogenous content of the soil. Alder makes good firewood when completely dry, and once alder charcoal was an important constituent of gunpowder. It is rarely used commercially nowadays, and anyway the alder trees found growing beside rivers and burns in the valley bottoms of hill country tend to be rather stunted, but the timber does not rot under water and makes good piles for bridges. Birch logs make excellent firewood too, and these logs show less difference in moisture content between fresh and dry wood than many other species, and can be burned green more readily. However birch timber is not a great deal of use except for small items like cotton reels and porridge spurtles, and sometimes for plywood. Both are comparatively quick growing trees, and are less attacked by rabbits in hard weather than most other species, although after a period of snow and hard freezing weather some young birches can be found with bark eaten off all round the base of the tree by rabbits, thus causing them to die eventually.

The last of the trees to come into leaf is the aspen, a member of the poplar family, which is mostly a native of the north. This beautiful tree rarely spreads

by seeding, for its seeds perish if they do not germinate quickly, and favourable conditions seem rarely to occur. However, as it is widespread in some areas, the trees must procreate by seed germination occasionally, for they are not especially long lived. However they do spread profusely by means of suckers, and given the opportunity a thicket of young aspens will grow up around mature trees to replace them in time. Unfortunately aspen seedlings are attractive to sheep, cattle and rabbits and opportunities for the young plants to grow unmolested are limited. Moreover, in hard winter weather rabbits will strip the bark from aspen seedlings, even ones that are several years old, and kill them, so that this beautiful tree has little chance to multiply. I am unaware that aspen bark has any particular properties, and imagine that it is stripped and eaten in the same way that rabbits will damage and destroy almost any young trees with tender bark when other herbage is covered by snow. Horses will strip the bark from quite large aspen trees, as they will also from rowans, so perhaps there is something that attracts them. It is said that horses and cattle will strip and eat willow bark when feeling unwell. Whether this is true I do not know, but of course aspirin is derived from salicylic acid, which is extracted from the *Salix* (willow) family of plants. Aspen leaves are remarkable for their constant fluttering in a breeze, due to the fact that they have long flattened leaf stalks. I am told that the Welsh name for aspens translates into something like 'the tree with leaves that flutter like a woman's tongue'! In autumn, after a hard frost, the lovely pale green aspen leaves turn into a remarkable range of colours from bright yellow to deep red, and many shades in between. The ground beneath an aspen tree after a frosty morning in late autumn, when the leaves are still damp and the colours at their best, is a truly amazing display of nature's beauty. I often collect a few of the fallen leaves of contrasting colour to marvel at them for a while, until in time they dry out and the colours fade from their best.

May is the time for getting ready for the summer those in-bye fields that are to produce root crops. Depending upon the opportunities provided by the weather, fields that are due for cultivation probably will already have been ploughed, and if conditions were suitable in April spring cereal crops will have been sown, but on some higher land this may not have been possible due to the pressure of lambing work on single-handed farms, or because the land has been too wet and cold. In such cases there is urgency to get the seed sown and the seedbeds rolled before warmer spring weather not only encourages germination, but may render seedbeds too dry for even germination. Turnip crops for the feeding of cattle and sheep the following winter will need to be sown. Many farmers still sow turnip seed on ridges, and then thin out the germinated turnip seedlings subsequently, at the same time as weeding the crop, by hand with a hoe; however, this labour-intensive system, originating from when the root crop in the rotation was the opportunity to reduce the weeds and clean the land, is gradually being replaced by growing turnips on the flat ground, as on southern farms, with the spacing of plants controlled by the sowing machinery, often combined with chemical weeding. Many smaller farms still grow turnips in the traditional way on ridges, though, entailing first heaping the soil into ridges with a ridging plough with double mould boards. A special sowing machine then deposits the turnip or swede seed on top of the ridge of soil, at intervals dictated by bands with holes carefully spaced in them, through which the individual seeds are forced, to drop onto the ground. A small wheel presses the seed into the soil on the ridge top. When the turnips or swede plants have germinated, another machine, called a scarifier, is pulled up the drills, and this peels off the outer layer of the soil ridge, together with any germinated weeds, leaving the turnip seedlings on top of a narrow, cleaner, ridge. These are singled with a hoe by hand in due course to destroy weed seedlings left on top of the ridges and to increase the spacing of the turnip plants by removing excess and poor ones, although on some bigger farms chemical weedkillers are applied to obviate hand hoeing and the seed spacing is greater.

Hayfields need preparation too. Growing hay is not merely a matter of shutting up a grass field and just letting it grow. Some fertilizer may need to be spread to make the grass grow more strongly, and to replace minerals taken off in previous crops. Any rabbit holes made in the field will need to be filled in, and if there has been a significant amount of mole activity the molehills may require to be spread with grass harrows, before the ground is consolidated with a heavy roller to improve the rooting system of the crop. During rolling any rabbit holes that were too large to fill in, rocks, or other obstacles, need to be marked with sticks that will be adequately visible to anyone mowing the tall hay subsequently, so that these can be avoided. Failure to do so could mean damaged machinery. On good farming land the idea of such obstacles in fields may seem strange, but in hill country these are quite normal. On this farm we have only two fields that do not have rocks protruding above ground to some degree, even after removal attempts by blasting, and in both of these it is a constant battle to reduce rabbit holes to a minimum, for even after filling in those visible in the spring the rabbits reopen them, or dig new ones during early summer in the cover of the hay. In one eight-acre field in which we used to grow a hay crop we had over thirty marker sticks, identifying rocks and rabbit holes, before we finally abandoned it for cropping hay and used it solely for grazing. Prior to this we had blasted a number of rocks to remove them, but some were simply too big for economical removal. The fight against the burrowing rabbits, by gassing and filling in the holes, was a losing one. Ploughing and reseeding is a very expensive operation, and certainly no guarantee against recolonization by rabbits, and in hill country permanent grassland has much merit, even where there is choice, because of its resistance to poaching in winter and to drying out in summer, as well as the better mineral content of the grazing due to more varied herbage and probably a greater content of forbs.

During May young rabbits can be seen sitting in groups at the mouths of nesting burrows in fine weather, especially during early morning and in the evenings, and the farmer knows that the cycle is starting again and soon there will be rabbits everywhere. Rabbits breed from March to September, but most of the young are born from about May to August. The ability of rabbits to multiply is legendary. Doe rabbits can breed up to five or six times a year, and produce a litter averaging about five young. However, this high optimum rate of reproduction is not likely to apply to all female rabbits. A doe rabbit can conceive at five months old, or earlier, and can become pregnant again within a few hours of giving birth, so that the breeding can be a constant process through the summer. The gestation period is about 30 days, and most does dig special short nesting burrows in which to give birth to their young. These nesting burrows are carefully hidden, with the entrances blocked, and the female rabbit makes a nest of grass and fur into which to deposit her blind and naked young. She visits the nest on average only once in twenty-four hours after giving birth, usually at night, and remains there for only about three minutes or so, perhaps a little longer initially when the babies are very small, giving the young just time enough to suckle her very rich milk. The baby rabbits open their eyes on the eleventh day, and their ears on the twelfth, and can stand on the thirteenth. After about three weeks the mother begins to be less particular about blocking the burrow entrance, and the babies start to emerge, and immediately eat grass. After about a month they are weaned, and the doe rabbit is no doubt by then preoccupied by the prospect of the arrival of the next litter.

Appreciation of the ability of rabbits to breed is likely to give rise to much concern to farmers, and to those living in the countryside where the rabbits may

gain access to their gardens. The classic example of a population running riot in conditions of plentiful food and lack of predators is of course the experience of the introduction of the rabbit into Australia in 1859. Twenty-four rabbits were introduced onto a property near Geelong in that year, and by 1865 over 20,000 had been killed on the estate! By 1883 the New South Wales government had spent large sums of money on trying to eliminate rabbits, killing almost 8 million of them. Apparently one man released thirteen rabbits onto his property in 1867, realized his mistake, and then spent £7000 in the following three years trying to eradicate them! However, the outcome of the breeding here is unlikely to achieve this alarming potential, for the odds are stacked against rabbit survival, with more predators and other dangers than in early Australian colonization. As with all animal populations, when these reach dangerously high levels for the wellbeing of the creatures themselves, the ability of the animals to breed deteriorates, embryos are resorbed, abortions may occur, or young may be left to starve.

The significance of rabbits to farmers can be illustrated by reference to the calculation that eight rabbits eat as much as one sheep. In the 1930s an estimate put the British rabbit population at 50 million, which was about four times the number of sheep. This figure almost doubled by the pre-myxomatosis 1950s. In 1990 the Ministry of Agriculture estimated that rabbits could be costing British farmers as much as £120 million a year in crop losses alone, and that if numbers continued to increase the loss could reach £400 million per annum. This does not take into account damage done to the environment, and to the attempts to improve this by tree planting, and so on. The cost to forestry is immense because of the absolute necessity of erecting rabbit netting around plantations, and the essential tree guards necessary for the planting of individual trees increases the cost dramatically. Even tree guards are no guaranteed protection in areas that have heavy snow falls in winter, for rabbits can sit on top of deep snow and chew trees above the level of all except the tallest tree guards, and they can also climb over conventional rabbit fencing at normal height, or bite holes in the wire, and in deep snow can get over the fence with ease.

Fortunately, the life expectancy of a rabbit is not high. Whereas a rabbit might live to eight years old or so in ideal conditions, its lifespan in the wild in this country is little more than two years. Predation, including that by man, takes a considerable toll, and few young rabbits survive to over a year old. Male rabbits themselves are aggressors, and a buck rabbit finding a nesting burrow is likely to dig it out and kill the young, whilst foxes, badgers and dogs destroy many young in this way. Others are drowned in burrows in wet weather. If the young rabbits survive until autumn they face the hazard of disease, which for centuries has taken a toll on the rabbit population sufficient to keep it below the out-of-control horror experienced in last century Australia. Myxomatosis, introduced deliberately in 1953, of course had a dramatic effect, killing well over 90 per cent of the rabbit population initially, and most people think of this as the factor governing population control. However, since the Normans introduced rabbits in the twelfth century hepatic coccidiosis, or liver rot, has been known to have occurred regularly, and this affects a high percentage of young rabbits, although those that survive develop immunity. In autumn a majority of young rabbits develop spots on their livers; some badly infected livers look like salami. These rabbits are invariably in poor condition and thin, and many die; others develop subsidiary diseases, such as yersiniosis, as a result of their weakened condition, and young rabbits with signs of diarrhoea are likely to be suffering from this and will die. Therefore coccidiosis is probably a factor controlling the explosion of the rabbit population, even though the effect of myxomatosis has waned, and apparently continues to do so. Over the past forty years since myxomatosis was introduced a degree of immunity has developed and strengthened, and these days it is common to see rabbits with scars around their eyes where clearly they have been exposed to the disease but recovered, and fewer pathetic mortally afflicted animals are seen as either immunity increases or the virus strains weaken. Young rabbits with livers affected by coccidiosis seem to be less common in very dry weather, and it is possible therefore that dry summers facilitate increase in the rabbit population.

Few farmers would care to see the countryside totally denuded of rabbits, as in the 1950s, but the current population, which will benefit from any increases in cover from policies such as set-aside in agriculture, is a major cost to farmers, both in loss of crops and loss of grazing for cattle and sheep, and in physical damage to fields with the excavation of holes. Thus the sight of baby bunnies sitting in the sun at the mouth of their nesting burrow may not be a welcome one for the farmer.

The yellow broom flowering on the hill is a cheerier sight, and the flowers are apparently regarded as tasty by the sheep as well as by deer. Although broom can spread rapidly, especially where soil has been disturbed, it serves the useful purpose of providing shelter for sheep and cattle, without the unpleasant prickles of gorse. Broom can be susceptible to hard weather, however, and severe winters can kill older bushes.

There is a saying that the farmer's boot is one of the best management tools. This does not refer to his application of this to helpers or employees, but to his walking about on the farm assessing the situation with regard to the grazing and crops. Raising cattle and sheep on grass is not merely a matter of putting the animals into a field for the summer and shutting the gate, perhaps then leaning on it at intervals to check that the animals are all thriving. Management of grazing is a skill. The management can affect both the constituents of the grassland and the quality of the feeding. Fields that are undergrazed become rank and weed plants flourish and the clover content is reduced as a result of the plants being overshadowed by the taller grass and other species. Ground that is overgrazed becomes bare and again allows less palatable species to grow, because the beasts prefer to graze down the more appetizing species. Research has shown, or rather confirmed what many farmers had realized from observation over the years, that the most productive grassland, and the one preferred by cattle and sheep, is where the herbage is maintained at a height of only a very few inches. Consequently it is important to move stock as appropriate in order to try to achieve this, so that their grazing alternates. Moreover all animals appreciate fresh grazing, and cattle

and sheep all welcome the opportunity to graze areas that have not had their own kind walking about on it for some days previously.

This policy of grazing management is as important on the open hill as in the fields, though obviously it differs somewhat, and it is impossible to confine sheep in certain areas when they are free to wander. Not surprisingly sheep on the hill tend to concentrate upon green areas of sweeter grass on patches of better soil or in damper areas. A good shepherd will try to disperse large concentrations of sheep in small areas, both to avoid these preferred grazing spots being denuded of grass, but also to lessen the inevitable build up of parasites and disease organisms in any place where beasts are feeding intensively. There is a natural tendency for sheep to move down the hill in the evenings to the sweeter grass in valley bottoms, feeding there overnight. This is possibly an atavistic trait inherited from times when grazers ventured down at night when it was safer from predators. A shepherd, with the aid of his dogs, will go round daily, encouraging the sheep to spread out back up the hill to try to ensure more even grazing and avoid the animals spending too much time in concentrated areas. A sheep's worst enemy can be another sheep, from the point of view of encouraging disease and parasites.

June

June sees the start of summer in the hill areas. The sun has warmth in it now, and indeed sometimes too much for some of the sheep it seems, for there are signs of their fleeces loosening around their necks and some of them losing wool, especially those that scratch on rocks or fences. On the lower ground some sheep will be seen to be shorn already, but in higher country clipping is later. We generally aim to try to have the clipping done during the second half of June. At this time of year the wool naturally reaches a point to facilitate discarding the previous year's growth, in the same way that all animals change from winter to summer coats. The wool on the sheep weakens at a point where a new level of growth starts – shepherds call this a 'rise'. Some sheep begin to look as though they are wearing loose-necked sweaters. Sheep that are unshorn gradually cast their old fleeces, sometimes in matted chunks of wool or quite large portions of fleece. Shearing is easier where this dividing line between old and new wool is evident, though in many low ground flocks, as in New Zealand, sheep are shorn twice a year; they are clipped before they are housed in early winter, both to avoid them becoming too warm in buildings, and so that they take up less room in pens.

At this time of year the farmer has to be specially watchful for sheep getting couped (stuck on their backs and unable to rise). Sheep can die very quickly when trapped thus, especially in warm weather, and it may be necessary to check the flock twice a day, particularly after heavy rain, for a sheep can die in the space of half a day in such conditions. A wet fleece is substantially heavier than a dry one, and most of the wool is on the sheep's back, so it is easy to understand how a thick fleece that is wet can not only anchor a sheep on its back, but can easily cause a sheep lying in a hollow or awkward position to be pulled onto its back and so get stuck. We have found ewes that were checked in the morning lying dead on their backs in a depression in uneven ground in the evening. So at this time of year one is anxious to see fleeces clipped for this reason alone, quite apart from problems with parasites and flystrike. With the sheep hot and itchy they are inclined to rub themselves, and wool is caught on trees, fence posts and other scratching points. They are also inclined to roll onto their backs to rub these on the ground, and of course this exposes them to great risk of being unable to right themselves and becoming couped.

In the old days the shearing of sheep was something of an event, and it still is to some extent on those farms with large sheep flocks. This was because many people were involved, both with gathering in the sheep, which is somewhat of a communal effort on the larger sheep farms with extensive areas of hill from which to collect the spread-out sheep flock, and in the actual shearing when this was all done by hand. These days with fewer shepherds looking after larger numbers of sheep, and so less men available, coupled with the declining number of shepherds and farmers able or prepared to shear, this job is mostly carried out by teams of shearers going round from farm to farm. It is a young man's job, even though there are still plenty of older shepherds shearing ably. Clipping is hard work and sore on the back, involving continual bending to work on the sheep. Sometimes fit young farmers' sons group together as a shearing team for the season, this being a way of earning extra money from a short period of hard work. These days we employ one such team to clip our sheep, and the job is easily completed in a day.

The critical factor with the organization of shearing is the weather. One cannot clip wet or damp sheep, and damp fleeces rot and will not keep. For farmers with large sheds there is less of a problem, for if rain seems likely they may be able to get the flock inside under cover and kept dry. However, this is not quite so straightforward, since the heavily fleeced sheep get hot and sweat in a building herded together. Damp sheep put inside in the hope that they will dry off will not do so properly unless they have plenty of space and fresh air, which requires a large building, and anyway they cannot be kept inside for any length of time without proper access to food and water. Not many hill farmers have suitable indoor facilities, and this means that much depends on getting dry weather, preferably with a slight breeze. Rain in one area, preventing the shearers from working on the farm scheduled for that day delays everyone, since this has obvious repercussions down the list of farmers waiting for their services. There may be some alternative farms with inside facilities, or where it has not rained, but even moving to work on these means packing up their equipment and travelling to another farm if rain interferes with the clipping, and this is not always practical; if it seems to be just a shower that halts clipping it may be more sensible simply to wait and hope that a breeze dries the sheep later in the day and enables clipping to proceed.

The result of this dependency on the weather is that in most seasons it is not only impossible to book the shearing team for a particular day, but it can be uncertain over a period as to when they may be able to finish shearing the sheep at farms earlier on the list and so come to one's own farm. The hill farmer is at a disadvantage in this respect, since the sheep in the hills become ready for clipping later than those in lower country or nearer the coast, and this means that the hill farmer is further down the queue, which has a cumulatively disproportionate effect on delays caused earlier in the season. Most shearing teams have many thousands of sheep to clip in a season, and organization is difficult. If the farm before one's own on their list has a large flock, they may not know which day they will finish clipping there in uncertain weather. We have had the shearers telephone at 11 o'clock at night, after we were in bed, to say that they would be there at 8 o'clock next morning! This meant an early rise next day to gather the sheep from a field where they had been put in readiness and have them in the pens and available for the clippers by 8 a.m.

In our case the clipping team consists of three young shearers, who bring a special trailer with them. This trailer has a race down one side of it, with three

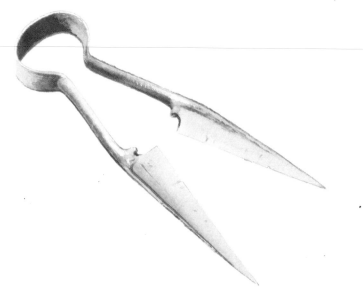

gates opposite where the shearers stand. It also has electrical connections for their clippers, and they carry a long extension wire to plug this into a source of electricity at the farm. Standing on the trailer to shear keeps the fleece clean. The person rolling the fleeces and packing them into the woolsacks removes each fleece as it is ready and the shorn sheep is released. On single-handed farms an extra person has to be employed to roll fleeces, but the shearing team may include a helper to do this. The race on the trailer is lined up with the sheep pens, with the aid of hurdles or gates, so that sheep may be driven into the race from the pens, and in order to keep the operation running smoothly the race on the trailer in front of the clippers has to be kept full. At the very front of the race is a small pen in which is put a decoy sheep at the start. Sheep seeing one ahead of them are more inclined to enter the race. As each shearer finishes clipping a sheep he can move away the shorn fleece with his foot and open the sprung gate in front of him and reach in and pull out another sheep to be clipped. The person rolling the fleece then removes this, rolls it, and puts it into the woolsack. The woolsacks are many times the size of a normal sack, capable of taking perhaps forty rolled fleeces, which have to be packed in very tightly. When the sack is full it is sewn shut with a large sack needle using thick string specially provided for the purpose. Prior to clipping several woolsacks are hung either on a special purpose-made framework, or on high gates or other convenient places, tied firmly at either end so that the fleeces can be packed down, if necessary by somebody climbing into the sack and tramping the wool.

The whole system works very satisfactorily on smaller flocks, but where there are larger sheep numbers the clippers may have catchers bringing them sheep instead of using the trailer. The men employed as catchers have to be fit and strong, for they are required to catch individual sheep in the pens and then take them out and pass them to the clippers as required.

June is the month when roe deer kids and red deer calves are born. Occasionally the hill farmer may come upon a little, spotted newly-born calf or kid curled up in a clump of rushes or heather. Like many other animals, deer mothers leave their offspring seemingly unattended for quite long periods. Cattle do the same with newly-born calves. This does not mean that the young deer are unattended, for the mother may not actually be far off but it is natural for all young animals to have long periods of rest between feeds, especially before they are large enough to be very active. All such young creatures should be left undisturbed. It is highly probable that they are not abandoned but that an anxious mother is nearby.

The coats of the adult deer are now changing, with the roe casting their insulated greyish winter coats and becoming the typical summer golden-red colour. Despite their name, red deer are not so reddish in colour as the little roe deer, though in certain light they can look it. Their longer coats are more of a light brownish grey. Shed hairs from their winter coats are often found where deer have been lying, and many birds appreciate these as nesting material. The earlier nesting birds will now have youngsters to tend and will be busily feeding these. One becomes aware that the cuckoo is silent, though not departed, and generally other birds are too busy feeding their young to spend as much time singing as earlier, and there is no longer need for territorial display. The curlew on the hill is silent, except when we go too near the nest site or young, when the parent birds will fly above us shouting loudly. In the hayfields, where the grass is growing tall, it provides good cover for ground nesting birds like the pheasant and partridge, and sometimes a mallard duck if the field is next to a burn or other water. Roe often have their kids in a hayfield, which provides fine cover and good feeding, but unfortunately they represent a problem, for the instinct of a frightened kid is to lie doggo. It is very difficult for a tractor-driver operating a mowing machine to see what lies in a thick hay crop, and many roe kids get killed in this way. Silage making, with a thicker crop, earlier cut, undoubtedly accounts for an even higher toll of young roe deer. The best way to try to obviate this unnecessary killing is to walk the field thoroughly with dogs the day before it is mown. Even if any kids present are not discovered, the disturbance and scent caused may prompt the doe to remove any kids to a safer place when all is quiet. Hopefully most young birds will be hatched and grown sufficiently to be able to fly out of harm's way when these fields are mown for a later cut hay crop.

Occasionally one may see and hear skylarks on hill ground where there is grass kept short by sheep, or on larger grazed hill fields, but many such song birds are getting rarer. We used to see skylarks commonly on our hill in past years, but sadly these days there are few to be seen and heard in early summer. On high hill tops in mountain country golden plover nest, and the shepherd walking the hill may disturb one of the pair and be greeted by their plaintive whistling call. On wetter parts of the hill snipe nest in tussocky areas, and in early summer their 'drumming' can be heard on still days from some distance away. This 'drumming' sound is often described as 'bleating', and from this was derived some of the various nicknames of the snipe, such as goat of the bogs or goat of the air. The noise is produced by the outer tail feather on each side, which is much stiffer than the other feathers and is held by the snipe so that it vibrates when the bird dives through the air. Although both male and female snipe have been shown to 'drum', the noise is nearly always made by the male in his display flight over his breeding territory. The snipe flies

around this at a considerable height, from time to time diving briefly to make this extraordinary, powerful noise that can carry a long distance, and then swooping upwards again to carry on the flight. Often on hill ground where a number of pairs of snipe nest one can see and hear several birds indulging in their drumming display flight at once. We have several pairs of snipe nesting on our hill each year and see and hear them often.

Sheep on the hill, where they are not grazed intensively or in large numbers, have a beneficial effect on the flowering of many short-growing plant species, by keeping the taller grasses and plants grazed down short enough to enable the smaller plants to have less competition and to flourish. Unfortunately sheep also like to eat the flowers too, so where sheep are removed from these areas during the flowering season an abundance of flowers such as orchids and rock roses proliferate where the soil is suitable. With the hill fenced into different compartments we try to alternate the sheep grazing, both for the benefit of the sheep, to give them fresh grazing periodically, especially for the young lambs, but at the same time to allow naturally flowering plants to complete their cycles. As a result of this policy we have at least eight varieties of orchid growing on the farm out of over 230 recorded plant species. These include the rare coralroot orchid that grows in association with birch roots, and has no leaves. The flowers are small and very difficult to spot in rushy or tussocky ground until one 'gets one's eye in' and can pick them out as a result of recognizing precisely what to look for on the ground. The coralroot orchid is apparently recorded in only about twenty areas of the country, but I suspect that it is actually present in many more places where the appropriate habitat exists. In some years the flowers appear in profusion for a few weeks, and in other years they are less abundant. The rare little white orchid has also been found on our farm and the fragrant orchid grows in thousands all over the hill on drier tussocks and harder ground. Its sweet scent is extremely powerful when experienced close up. On the wetter ground various other orchids grow in profusion during June and July.

Over much of the flatter parts of our hill *Trollius*, the globeflower, grows in abundance, where the ground is not too wet. These flowers are like tall oversized buttercups, of a slightly paler yellow, and they can be readily spotted amongst buttercups. Some people call *Trollius* 'butterballs', which the flowers certainly resemble. In some places there are bright yellow patches of *Trollius* clearly visible from the farm down below, providing a spectacular display, with flowers quite as big as cultivated varieties.

A less welcome plant to farmers in some areas, but ubiquitous in wet ground in the north, is the pretty bog asphodel, with its lovely, yellow, starry flower spikes in June followed by attractive reddish seedheads in August. In one place I spotted from a distance a clump of pale yellow flowers that seemed unfamiliar. When I got up close I found that it was a small, but apparently gradually expanding patch of pale yellow bog asphodel growing on a tussock and spilling down onto the wet peat below. Even the seed pods are recognizably much paler than normal. This patch grows every year and I always visit it in summer since I find the colour variation of interest, these being the only pale plants that I have seen out of thousands. The leaves of the bog asphodel eaten under certain photosynthetic conditions of sunlight can cause an ailment in sheep called 'yellowses', as can St John's wort, which grows on slightly drier ground but not in such quantity. This condition and its precise cause is not clearly understood, but the result is to make sheep, especially white-faced ones, photosensitive on unprotected areas of the body, such as their ears, which swell up and become oedematous, possibly oozing a yellowish fluid that encrusts on them. Some farmers house these affected sheep in a dark building and may slit their ears to release the fluid, but in due course the skin is sloughed off and the affected areas regenerate and return to normal. 'Yellowses' is not common, and only affects some sheep, and then apparently only in certain photosynthetic conditions. Nevertheless it is an example of the sort of problem for which the hill farmer and shepherd, particularly in the north of the country, has to be on the outlook.

This is the time of the year for the hatching of poultry young in the farmyard. These days proper free-range farmyard poultry are less common, and many town dwellers, or people that use only shop-bought eggs, have no idea of the deep orange-yellow colour of the yolks of eggs from hens reared naturally on self-chosen diets of green plants, seeds and insects, neither have they experienced the superb taste of chicken from birds reared thus. Hens, and bantam hens in

particular, that are allowed to wander at will, frequently prefer to nest naturally in bushes or clumps of undergrowth, which can be tiresome when the farmer's wife may require the eggs for eating. The observant farmer, or, more usually, farmer's wife, probably discovers nesting sites, either by looking in appropriate or favoured places, or by watching the hens to see to where they go, or from where they emerge. However, every now and again a bird disappears and reappears, either hurriedly at feeding time, when a little corn may be thrown in the yard for the poultry as a supplement, clucking and clearly broody, or three weeks later with chicks. If it is a duck, goose or turkey that disappears to sit on eggs it will be rather longer before they reappear of course, for the incubation period of duck and turkey eggs is 28 days against 21 for hen eggs, and geese may be a couple of days longer. Surprisingly, that of Muscovy ducks is longer still at 35 days. Muscovy ducks, of course, are actually of the goose rather than the duck family. Our turkeys seem to like nesting in the ivy on top of the stone dykes round the garden, near where they roost at night on the roof of a small shed and in the lower branches of a small pine tree and the big ash tree.

The raising of poultry in the farmyard is not always simple. Hens, and especially bantams, are usually attentive and ferocious mothers, brooding their chicks frequently, and defending them from predators as best they can. However, other poultry can be less satisfactory, and rats can be a tremendous problem. Rats are attracted by poultry food, and also by water. In summer rats, which can swim well, even under water, often follow, or live by, watercourses such as wet ditches, streams and burns, and most hill farms have streams or a duckpond or other watercourse nearby. Rats seem to be attracted particularly to goslings, and will kill them even when quite large. Even a hen is no sure protection for a gosling, since despite these being so large as to be barely able to be brooded by a hen, a rat will tunnel underneath a run if it can and literally eat out the guts of the gosling beneath the hen overnight. Rats also seem to be attracted to the frequent squeaking of turkey chicks, and any that stray far from their mother or foster mother are at great risk. We put down poisoned rat bait in poultry-proof tunnels, but this is not a complete answer to the problem. Crows, rooks and other aerial predators are also a great danger to young ducklings and very young goslings. Many of these can only be raised successfully consistently by means of a good foster mother hen, and kept in a run small enough for the hen to defend, until the youngsters are old enough to be safe. The increasing sparrowhawk population also takes its toll of young birds, and, as much as we like to see these raptors, and welcome the increase in their numbers to previous levels, further expansion of their population might well become problematical.

Young chicks can suffer from hypothermia in just the same way as lambs, only the cause is more due to heat loss than lack of food. They need constant brooding to keep up their body temperature initially. We had a bantam sitting on fifteen eggs high up on a stack of hay bales. I wondered if she might have difficulty in

getting her chicks all down safely from a height of about 4.5m. One day she appeared in the farmyard with two tiny chicks. I got a ladder and went to check the nest, for I felt that she probably had been sitting on more eggs than that. Sure enough I found in her nest the remains of the two eggs that had hatched, nine unhatched eggs, and four chicks of various colours lying around on their backs. I removed these corpses, intending to give them to the ferrets, but as I crossed the yard I saw a slight movement in one of them. Careful watching suggested that another was also not completely dead. So I took all the chicks and placed them in the bottom oven of the cooker where they would get a gentle heat. A few minutes later all four had their eyes open and were squeaking, including one that I had felt sure was dead. So I took them out into the yard and returned them to the bantam hen. She flew at me when they squeaked and she saw my hand near them. Then she settled down to brood, calling the chicks to her. The weak ones managed to struggle to her underneath a trailer in the middle of the yard, but the smallest seemed unable to get below her in amongst the warm feathers and merely stuck its head in below her. Later I went to check them and found to my delight that all the chicks had survived except the smallest one.

Rooks are a constant problem, being inveterate egg stealers, as well as being quite prepared to take young chicks. Although rooks do the farmer a service for a good part of the year in destroying large quantities of wireworms and other agricultural pests, this benefit can seem to be outweighed by the constant thieving of the food put out for sheep or hens, and the taking of eggs and young poultry, as well as being a danger to very young lambs. One day I watched a rook pursuing a very young rabbit, pecking at it. The baby bunny was not able to run fast, being not long emerged from its nest burrow, and the rook easily kept pace. However I felt sorry for the young rabbit and frightened the rook away, and the bunny retreated down a hole. Cereal farmers suffer damage on laid crops at harvest time from rooks, and these birds will also dig up and damage seed potatoes. Nevertheless rooks have a certain attraction strutting about the fields in their glossy black plumage, and they can put on displays of thrilling aerobatics that seem amazing and incongruous to their usual slow flapping flight. Crows and magpies are a problem for poultry too, and if they locate a nest they will systematically rob it. One year a turkey decided to nest in the broom on the burn bank, but her nest was rather exposed and was easily spotted by the magpies. I tried camouflaging the nest, and even built a structure over it to protect it, but the magpies still stole or ate each egg as it was laid. Finally the turkey went broody, figuring that she had laid enough, and sat tightly, unfortunately on nothing! When I blocked the nest so that she could not get into it and sit there

she merely went and sat beside it, so I gave up and let her get on with it. She only did this for a couple of days before abandoning the idea.

On the ponds the young blackheaded gulls have hatched by this time, and walking anywhere nearby the colony produces a screeching cloud of angry and alarmed adult gulls swooping overhead. On the quieter ponds, where there are no gull colonies, the damselflies and dragonflies are active. The damselflies flit about, pairing and laying eggs at the water's edge, with the different coloured adults flying about paired together, or singly seeking mates. The larger dragonflies zoom round their territories at great speed, and then hover like marvellous miniature live versions of helicopters. The dragonflies are fierce carnivores and prey on all manner of insects, including mosquitoes, midges and horseflies. Unlike damselflies, which flit low round the shallow edges of ponds in quite large numbers, dragonflies are territorial and defend their territories, although these may vary and not be maintained for more than a few days. Damselflies are not so territorial. The lifespan of dragonflies and damselflies is short. In fact many live little more than a week after maturity, but those that survive this may live to between three and seven or eight weeks on occasion. Dragonflies are one of our fastest, and largest, insects, and fascinating to watch when on patrol.

There is plenty to see, and much to learn, around the farm, but there is always much work to be done too. A good deal of farming seems to consist of mending things. If not machinery, then there always seem to be fences to repair. Sheep are adept at finding holes in or under fences, and, if they so wish, they can wriggle underneath surprisingly small gaps. Of course when directed to return whence they came they invariably refuse to attempt this. A determined sheep can force its way through even a nine-line wire fence, particularly those in hard and rocky or wet ground, where it is impossible to tighten the wires as taut as the books advise to be completely stockproof! Heavy duty stockfence netting is the only certain way of keeping sheep inside, or out from, a field, and this has to be erected as tight as possible and without any small gaps underneath. Unfortunately cattle sometimes rub on these fences and loosen, or break, fence posts, and they have to be hammered in tightly again, or replaced, from time to time. The repair of fences can appear to be a never-ending task on a farm at times. Stockfence netting can have disadvantages too in early summer, for whilst it can be an effective barricade against sheep, invariably lambs are tempted to reach through the square holes to nibble fresh grass on the other side, and sometimes, particularly horned lambs, find that having pushed their head through they cannot pull it back again, especially since they seem to have a tendency to push forward rather than pull back when caught by the head. Where sheep are enclosed with fencing of this type, checks have to be made regularly to ensure that all is well in this respect.

One of the frequent ailments to which sheep are prone is foot rot. Although lameness in sheep may be due to scald, which is a soreness between the cleaves, or to injury – an abscess, or occasionally even to a sharp stone or some such in the hoof – the most likely cause is foot rot. This is caused by a bacterium infecting the foot, causing part of the hoof to rot away, producing an evil-smelling sore. Foot rot is highly contagious, and can remain infective in soil for long periods. It is widespread throughout the sheep-rearing world. Attempts have been made to produce vaccines to assist in its eradication, but results have not been impressive.

Treatment consists of paring away the infected part of the hoof and exposing the area to the air, avoiding cutting the foot itself, and then treating it with antibiotic spray, or standing the sheep in a footbath containing formaldehyde solution for a short time, which also assists in hardening the foot. Very few sheep flocks, particularly on those farms with damp ground, escape foot rot infection in varying degree. Severe outbreaks can be back-breaking work for a farmer, who has to catch and upturn the sheep, and hold them whilst stooping to pare and treat the hooves. Even getting sheep into pens in order to treat some of them can be a tedious and lengthy operation, and it has always to be remembered that stress can be a significant factor in triggering off other problems, especially those where the organisms responsible are carried normally in the guts of healthy sheep, such as those which cause pasteurellosis, one of the main causes of sheep death. This can lead to ewes or lambs being found dead for no apparent reason. The stress of being handled in pens, such as dipping and dosing, or loaded into lorries, can trigger off pasteurellosis, especially in lambs and if there has been unusually warm or wet weather, and for this reason it is advantageous to keep the handling of the flock to a minimum compatible with good care.

One of the seemingly unending jobs of the hill farmer, especially in permanent grassland, is trying to get rid of various weed plants, of which thistles are one of the most notable. In bad infestations these can be sprayed quite effectively with herbicide where ground is flat enough for tractor use, but not only is selective weedkiller chemical expensive, but often these sprays check the growth of valuable clover too. Moreover not all farmers approve the use of chemical sprays on their land, and it is quite likely that thistles occur in steep hill areas where spraying by machine would be difficult or impossible anyway. In these circumstances trying to eradicate these weeds by hand is the only alternative. Some farmers prefer to scythe the thistles when they are almost full grown. The problem is that at the stage where the flower head has formed the cut plant will often continue to produce its downy seeds to blow around the farm. An alternative, that I prefer, is to spud the young plants as I walk round the farm checking the beasts daily. Spudding is carried out with a small angled blade on the end of a stick, with which the root is cut underground and the thistle plant removed clear of the soil. If not cut properly, or if shoots are left, these will grow and the plant will regenerate. I have the spudder on the end of a long stout stick, and I cut thistle plants with it daily as I walk round the farm, carrying out the job gradually during June and early July before the stems get tough when the plants start to mature ahead of seeding. It is tedious work but if carried out regularly is effective in reducing spear thistles, and then keeping control of new infestations. Other types of thistle, such as creeping thistle, which grows in patches, sometimes dense, are less easy to control by spudding, and these may have to be cut by scythe or mower before they flower, with this treatment repeated regularly to weaken the plant systems, which spread underground.

June is a quiet month with the cattle on the farm. There is plenty of grass and they graze contentedly, with the calves growing apace. Apart from checking daily that all is well with them, and moving them into fresh grazing fields from time to time as the grass length and availability dictates, there is little required in the way of management, which is as well at a time when the sheep involve much work. After the ewes are shorn it is easier to see which of these are still milking well or have udders damaged in some way, and any sheep with problems can be marked when they are in the pens and segregated with other problem ewes marked at lambing time for casting and selling when appropriate. The traditional time for the sale of cast ewes and feeding sheep is in the autumn, but those scheduled to go for slaughter as being unsuitable for breeding are sold at a time that is dependent both on current prices and grazing availability.

June days are long in the north, and the growth of vegetation is in full vigour. Where there are rowan and hawthorn trees, the air is often heavy with the sweet scent of their flowers. With the cattle grazing peacefully and the ewes contentedly feeding on the hill and their lambs growing apace, June can be a pleasant month for the hill farmer, with the trials of winter temporarily forgotten, and the worries about the hay crop and the weather for haymaking still a while ahead, although the stock still have to be checked regularly. We restrict the sheep to certain areas of the hill at this time of year, where they do not damage the wildflowers, for this is the main flowering period. Parts of it are yellow with *Trollius*, or globeflowers, showing up tall and paler against a backround of buttercups of different kinds, and the grassland on the flatter area is dotted with bright crimson mountain clover, yellow rattle, vetches, blue speedwells and a variety of orchids. In the damp areas cotton grass is beginning to seed and the long downy hairs appear to form the white cottony balls, that once were laboriously collected in some places for stuffing pillows or cushions. Also on damp, boggy ground the sundews are beginning to show their little spikes of tiny white flowers. This plant lives on the midges and small insects that alight on the dew-like drops of moisture at the end of the red hairs with which the leaves are covered. The insects are trapped by these sticky drops and the leaves gradually curl over and engulf them. The leaves then exude digestive juices that enables the plant to absorb the nutrients in the victim's body. Unfortunately even when sundews are abundant they make no noticeable inroads into the midge population. Butterwort is another insect-eating plant that grows in damp places on our hill, with the attractive blue violet-coloured flowers, hence its other name of bog violet. The leaves are sticky to insects, which become trapped, and their struggles cause the leaves to curl inwards over the victims, and then enzymes are secreted that digest the insects' bodies.

July

July is hay month on the hill farm. On lower ground farms the hay is long since made and much of it stacked in the barn ready for winter, but on higher ground the grass grows later and the hay is not ready to cut until later in the season. On many farms silage is made these days, or increasingly big-bale silage wrapped in plastic, in desperation at the difficulties of making hay because of the weather. However there are beginning to be signs that not everyone is happy with silage, both from the aspect of its quality as a feed, its cost and its effect upon the environment. The disadvantage of silage is that it involves heavy dressings of nitrogenous fertilizer. This is increasingly expensive, and much of the nitrogen evaporates into the air or is leached out into waterways anyway. The grass growth forced by heavy applications of nitrogen tends to be deficient in certain minerals, and this can be seen in young cattle fed inside in winter on heavily fertilized silage and barley, which tend to have pale rings round their eyes, denoting copper deficiency. Heavy fertilizer dressings to encourage thick early silage favours those grasses that respond best to such treatment, with the result that the crop tends to become almost a sort of monoculture. The early cutting is a danger to nesting

birds, young roe deer, hares and other creatures invisible in the thick grass and unseen by the operator of the forage harvester, and at a much younger stage of growth than at hay time so unable to flee destruction.

Many farmers, and others, appear to think that silage is the perfect answer to harvesting grass, and that the feed thus produced for cattle and sheep must be good quality. However, as with all other crops, the quality and feeding value of silage varies considerably, and just as much as does the feed value of hay. Moreover, poorly made silage produces a devastatingly potent polluting effluent, the disposal of which creates problems. Some people believe that this effluent can be fed to cattle. Other by-products have been fed to animals in the past, such as recycled poultry manure and even cattle manure, as well as the ground-up remains from slaughter houses, processed into cattle feed. Some of these practices have led to disastrous repercussions. The idea of feeding highly polluting silage effluent to animals does not seem appropriate, whatever the theoretical chemical content.

A modern development has been the making of big-bale silage, made possible by the introduction of big balers that can wrap grass at a stage which could not be handled by the previous small balers. The big baler operates on the principle of the old, small, round balers, that are now rarely seen. Unlike square balers that slice hay or straw into lengths and compress it into blocks, which are then bound with string, the round balers simply wind the grass or straw into a roll and finally encircle this with string or fine plastic netting to tie the bale together. The advantage is that the hay or straw wound round in layers presents a more weatherproof surface, especially if net-wrapped but the round bales cannot be packed inside a building as tightly as square ones. Round balers can collect and wind into a roll even damp green material, and so can handle grass cut as silage. The principle of silage making is that the material is preserved in airtight conditions and anaerobic changes take place. Normally made silage is preserved in specially made clamps, packed down to exclude air, and then covered as rapidly as possible with an airtight cover. This process can be achieved with big bales by enclosing them with a plastic covering, and the three methods of doing this are either by putting the bale into a plastic bag and closing and tying the open end, or placing the bales into a long plastic tube, like a sausage, and tying the end when it is full, or alternatively wrapping the bale tightly with a type of clingfilm plastic that completely covers it. With this method of silage making, not only is a silage clamp or pit not required, but the baled silage can be stored *in situ* ready for winter feeding, and the bales can be transported and placed in feeding containers. There are two main disadvantages however, apart from the extra expense. The first is that any damage to the plastic covering, such as chewing by rabbits or rodents for instance, can introduce air and cause part or all of the bale to rot. The second point is that the black plastic covers a lot of very poor silage, made easily perhaps, but sometimes without due care, and often made as a second choice when it is too wet for any other method of conserving!

The wrapping in plastic involves significant expense, and the handling of wrapped bales is more difficult since this has to be done with special machinery to avoid puncturing the plastic and introducing air to spoil the anaerobic silage within. Thus bales that are plastic wrapped can only be easily transported on the tractor's front loader spikes immediately prior to feeding and removal of the plastic altogether.

Some people are now beginning to realize that silage in general, but especially that made in plastic, is not a cheap feed, and very often not a good one, with the added disadvantage that it is not what some now describe as 'environmentally friendly'! Although some hill farmers make silage, and a few make big-bale silage as well as hay, most continue to make hay, since their fields are unlikely to be sufficiently productive to respond to high fertilizer applications in order to produce heavy silage crops, let alone several cuts in a season, and also if they are single-handed, silage making is not possible without hiring help or a contractor, since it requires another operator to be present either to pack down the freshly cut silage transported into the clamp or pit, or to assist with the covering of the big bales with plastic. Although many seasons militate against the making of good quality hay, it is still usually possible to make a conserved winter feed of satisfactory quality for hill cows, and for the sheep with more particular feeding preferences, in most seasons. Bad hay is actually dangerous, because moulds forming in damp hay release spores that cause farmer's lung, a disease that causes flu-like symptoms. Farmer's lung is a cumulative disease that damages the lung tissue and can be seriously debilitating. The modern, big round bales cannot be stacked tightly in a barn as were the small square bales, and so drying the hay mechanically with a high-powered blower to force warm air through the hay, is no longer possible. On the other hand the big round bales are more weatherproof and do not require immediate stacking in the field to be comparatively rainproof, and a great deal of hard work is thus saved. Those farms without substantial buildings for hay storage can stack the big bales outside with comparatively little loss due to weather if a cover is placed securely over the stack. However, big bales are perhaps more likely than small bales to heat inside and generate mould on account of the larger volume of hay compressed together.

When one considers that hill farmers may start supplemental feeding of hay as early as October to support the dwindling grass in the fields, when the feed value of the herbage is deteriorating, and are probably full feeding in November or early December, and will continue until May, one can appreciate the importance of the hay crop to them. Good hay is one of the best and most palatable feeds for cattle and sheep, as well as being the most natural. Home-made hay is also one of the most economical feeds. Consequently it is likely to be the most important crop on a hill farm, if not the only crop on some higher farms.

The haymaking operation may take anywhere between four or five days and even up to a month to complete, dependent entirely on the weather, but the quicker that it is made the better quality the hay is likely to be, if it was at the correct stage for cutting when mown, and if it was properly dry before being baled. In kind, sunny weather with a warm breeze, and no rain during the process, we are able to mow the hay and leave it to dry for three or four days, or longer if the weather looks likely to remain favourable, and then simply gather the crop up into fluffed-up rows ready for baling; but in unfavourable, wet weather we sometimes are unable to touch the hay for three weeks after mowing, or have to continually turn it to dry before baling can be considered. In these circumstances the hay turns out to be poor quality. Even should the chemically tested feeding value be reasonable, dictated largely by the stage at which the crop is cut, the palatability may have deteriorated as a result of exposure to weather, or to leaf loss from continual handling. When the hay lies cut for a long period, because wet weather prevents haymaking proceeding, the problem arises of new grass and clover growing up through the cut swathe. This not only prevents the cut crop from drying, but makes it difficult to rake up the hay into rows and inevitably leads to a significant loss of some of the crop.

The objective in haymaking is to try to get the grass as long and thick as possible, to maximize the quantity, but with the optimum feeding value, and yet not too difficult to cure. Once grass commences flowering, with subsequent seed formation, its feed value drops, and so the optimum time for cutting hay is when the grass flowerheads have emerged but the plants have not yet started to flower. The problem with the judgement of the best time for cutting is not a straightforward one, of course, since a field will contain not only a range of differing growth stages of grass of the same species, but also a variety of different grass species all at varying stages of growth. Thus the farmer has to endeavour to judge the most favourable time for mowing when the optimum quantity of the grass is at the appropriate stage, and in the context of the likely weather over the following week or fortnight. Once cut, the aim is to get the hay as dry as rapidly as possible, so that it can be baled and secured from the effect of the weather to maintain its goodness. The old saying 'make hay when the sun shines' is absolutely correct. There is no doubt that hay is better quality and more easily cured when made in a sunny period. The ideal is to have a warm breeze too, which can blow through the crop. A very thick crop of hay is more difficult to dry because the drying air cannot circulate freely through a thick-cut swathe, and this will necessitate turning the swathe over to allow the underneath to dry as well. At one time the advice was to continually turn the hay to allow this to dry as quickly as possible by constant exposure to the air. This may be appropriate for young grass in ideally warm, dry weather, but the problem is that as the hay dries the components become brittle, especially the more leafy parts of the grasses and the clover, which are the most valuable nutritious constituents, and the more the hay is handled the greater are the losses in the field. Accordingly the minimum of handling is desirable when conditions permit. In the past hay tended to be made

later in the season, when it was more easily cured; the hand-made crop was cured by hanging it on fences or structures made for the purpose, and was often of good feeding value and palatability, as a result of its containing a high proportion of the original leaves of the grasses and herbs, which are the most valuable part of the crop, even if cut at a later stage.

The current mood of encouraging extensification in stock rearing, not just in cattle and sheep but in pigs and poultry too, and the feeling that the inputs of nitrates and nitrogen products should be reduced, may see a return to the hay meadows of the past, where the grass crop is not heavily fertilized, and where permanent meadows provide a richer mixture of herbs and other forbs with the grasses.

Hayfields have become a topic in environmental conservation matters recently. Some older people recall with nostalgia these old permanent hay meadows, that contained a considerable mixture of grasses, herbs and wildflowers, partly because they were not heavily fertilized with artificial manure, and partly as a result of being cut a little later, allowing the later flowering plants to develop. Later mowing also allowed the creatures reared in the hayfields, such as young pheasants and other birds, leverets and roe kids, to grow larger and thus more able to escape destruction by the mowing machine. At the time of silage cutting or very early hay crops many birds are still sitting on eggs and being reluctant to flee from the machine are slaughtered by the mower. This early mowing has had a disastrous effect upon the now rare corncrake population, currently found only in very localized parts of the west coast of Scotland and Ireland, but comparatively widespread in times past.

The decision as to the suitability of the hay crop for baling is a critical one, because hay that is not completely dry causes problems in the bales. Moisture in the leaves and stems causes the sugars to ferment, and this results in the hay sweating and producing an ideal environment for the growth of fungi and moulds. Heated bales can be so hot that it is impossible to hold one's hand inside them, and a neighbouring farmer told me that one year, with terrible weather at hay time, his bales were too damp, and when stacked in a building they generated great heat such that he was unable to hold his hand on the outside of the concrete walls, and his wife was talking of calling the fire brigade! In fact there was no disaster, and in due course the hay cooled, and was used later for winter feed, though undoubtedly it would have been 'dusty'. Hay that has heated, and allowed moulds to form, is a health hazard to both farmer and livestock. These moulds and fungi produce spores, and when the hay is handled these form a dusty cloud with an unpleasant smell. The spores that are inhaled damage the lungs (farmer's lung), and this damage is permanent and so cumulative, even though the initial flu-like symptoms of infection may last only two or three days. Similar problems can also be precipitated in livestock inhaling the spores, especially those fed mouldy hay inside a building with little ventilation; so it is important to avoid baling hay that is not properly cured and sufficiently dry.

Thus it can be appreciated that hay time is an important and worrying time for the farmer, and particularly for those, such as hill farmers, that are completely reliant upon the hay crop for the winter food supply for their livestock, with the weather critical, a major factor in determining not only the ease or difficulty with which the hay is made, but also the final quality of the product.

July is the time when the young deer can be seen on the hill and in the woods. In the early mornings, perhaps walking round to check livestock, one can often see a roe deer doe with a kid following behind her, feeding in open patches between the birch trees, or crossing the road, and on the hill the red deer hinds that were at breeding stage in the previous autumn now mostly have calves at their side in the mornings and evenings. Often during the daytime the young of both species remain hidden, curled up in a clump of reeds or heather, while the adults leave them to continue feeding. This is quite normal, and both cattle and sheep also leave their youngsters to sleep off a good feed whilst curled up in shelter, and graze away from them, sometimes even on the far side of the field. Unfortunately many people do not understand this, and occasionally a walker or hiker may come across a roe deer kid or a red deer calf curled up, lying completely still, with no parent in sight, and think that the poor little creature has been

abandoned or its mother met with some disaster, whereas this is most unlikely. People should never handle young, wild animals thus found, for the human scent inevitably left will alarm the parent. Interference with nature should be avoided always, except in quite incontrovertible circumstances, which the layman may not be competent to judge. In the case of cattle or sheep that are not frightened of humans the mother may come running quickly to her offspring if she sees a person near it, and indeed a maternal cow can be quite dangerous at times, but a timid deer is likely to be too frightened to challenge a human examining her young. These young creatures instinctively lie motionless, and such behaviour is not a sign of tameness, although some inexperienced people might mistake it for this. It cannot be emphasized sufficiently strongly that wild creatures should never be meddled with, nor young animals handled, except by people knowledgeable of their ways who have good reason to do so. One of the few wild animals that responds to offerings of food without apparent fear is the hedgehog, which will often lap up a saucer of milk put in front of it, or consume a small quantity of chopped meat without fuss, especially when foraging hungrily in autumn before the arrival of the cold weather and hibernation.

The blackheaded gulls are attracted by the newly-mown hayfields. Blackheaded gulls are not sea-birds in the summer, for they nest inland, beside lochs

and ponds where reedbeds and rushes provide suitable nesting sites, and they remain inland until the young birds are fully grown. New-mown hayfields provide a good supply of corpses as well as insects on which they can feed, for inevitably some rabbits are killed by the mowing machine, and numbers of small voles and mice; also undoubtedly many slugs and insects are exposed to view and predation with the removal of the grass cover. The gulls follow the mower, hunting for titbits, and they continue to forage around the hayfields for some days thereafter. One day I watched blackheaded gulls continually swooping down and picking up a small dark object, and then flying to their cruising height and dropping it again. After seeing this occurrence repeated a number of times by different gulls I decided to see what was the object of their attention, which they clearly decided was distasteful. The next time that a gull picked it up I watched carefully and marked where it dropped the object and I went across and retrieved it. I found a dead mole. I was aware that birds, and many predators, find a mole distasteful, and this seemed to bear it out. I wondered whether the mole had a smell that the gulls found unpleasant perhaps, since they discarded it without ever trying to eat it. Both herons and buzzards will eat moles if given the opportunity of catching them at times when other food may be scarce, but many other predators will not do so even should they kill them.

On warm evenings, when it is almost dark, the blackheaded gulls can be seen, and heard, flapping slowly around the farmyard and across the fields, as they hunt

for moths. Insects make up a substantial proportion of the diet of blackheaded gulls in their breeding grounds. Once the young are old enough and with much of their full adult plumage, the gulls depart for the coast, and soon after hay time they disappear, and the only gulls then seen are a few herring gulls on stormy days when conditions at the coast are rough, and occasionally the huge blackbacked gulls that feed on the carcases of dead rabbits and other carrion, but have been known to kill newly-born lambs in spring.

Most of the young birds are now maturing and the swallow second broods are hatching. Swallows are sometimes regarded as a good guide to the weather, though in reality it is more likely that it is their food supply, the flying insects, that govern this, for swallows fly high in good weather, and presumably high pressure, but swoop low over the fields in poor weather when the barometric pressure is low.

In the early part of the month the gorse is in full bloom, although odd bushes can be found partially in flower in almost any month of the year. Gorse provides nesting shelter for a number of small bird species, but it also provides ideal cover for rabbits, as well as food for them in bad weather. In areas of high rabbit populations the gorse bushes are all trimmed at the level at which rabbits can feed. Some gorse offers windbreak shelter for cattle and sheep on the hill in winter, but large thickets are deleterious for the farmer, and perhaps for wildlife generally when it reduces the herbage variety by spreading into impenetrable clumps. The thickets are too dense for other plants to grow below the gorse bushes, so these die out. Cattle can be difficult to find on the hill when hidden in gorse thickets, whilst the prickles that get into the fleeces of the sheep make these extremely unpleasant to handle subsequently, since the shepherd can get these prickles into his hands from the wool. So one job of the hill farmer is to try to reduce the spread of gorse to a manageable level. On much of rough ground the only practical way to do this is by burning, but this is only a short-term measure, for much of the burned gorse regenerates from the roots or remaining stumps in due course. Burning time is in late winter, well before nesting birds might be thinking of using the cover, and it is best carried out after or during a hard frost with a gentle breeze. Gorse flares up spectacularly, producing an enormous blaze, and burning significant patches of it has to be carried out with considerable care to ensure that the fire does not get carried away and burn more than anticipated, especially in the vicinity of woodland. Gorse, or whin, has a high protein content and once was used as a winter stock feed, crushed to destroy the prickles before it was given to stock. There used to be special whin-crushing machinery sold for this purpose. The high protein content may account for the attraction of burnt gorse twigs to cattle, which readily eat these after a fire if given the opportunity.

The linnets, redpolls and goldfinches that fed on the dandelion seeds in the hayfields in early June, when the grass was still low, now turn their attention to groundsel and thistles and other plants that are seeding. Flocks of these birds are now rarer in many parts of the country, especially in the south, where more intensive agriculture and spraying of weeds has reduced the wild plants that are their food supply. Fortunately for these seed-eating birds many hill farms still have rough pastures that are uncultivated, or not intensively farmed, where their food plants can grow. Thistles are a pest on many upland farms, and their seeds blow considerable distances so they are difficult to eradicate. Even after diligent spudding of thistles earlier in the season young plants appear later in the year, and there always seems to be an unending succession of them throughout the growing season. Spudding spear thistles and marsh thistles kills those plants, but this is not practical with patches of creeping thistle. All of these, but especially the spear thistle, are favoured by goldfinches, and it is some compensation for the annoyance of the thistles in the fields to see the bright, almost tropical, colours of the goldfinches on the plants in rough ground where spudding has not been done, and to hear their cheerful, characteristic, tinkling call. Butterflies and bumblebees favour thistle flowers too. On the hill one can glimpse occasionally the bobbing white rump patches of the wheatear on rocks and old stone dykes, and in the fast-flowing burns and streams the charming dipper is often seen bobbing up and down on a rock or skimming low over the water in rapid flight; a sign that at least there is insect life in the water for its food supply, and that therefore the burn is comparatively unpolluted by acid rain.

July is the time for wild roses to bloom, on harder ground on the hill, where they have been protected from sheep and deer, and along the field sides and on

the farm tracks where there has also been protection from browsing. Many of the wild roses are on tall, thick, woody stems, as a result of young shoots lower down being browsed. There are a number of varieties, and four or five of these are to be found in hill country in the north. The situation is complicated by possible hybridization, but three types are quite easily identified because there are both pink- and white-flowered wild roses, and one pink variety with quite downy or hairy leaves. The dog rose may be pink or white, but the field rose is always white. The downy rose is mostly a deeper pink, and the leaves clearly downy. The dog rose probably gained its name as a result of the early Greeks believing that the roots were a cure, or help, if one was bitten by a mad dog. In more modern times children were given rose hip syrup, made from its hips, and rich in vitamin C.

If July is warm and then there is a wet spell, as often happens at the beginning of the month, we keep an eye out for horse mushrooms growing in the fields. These large mushrooms, far more delicious than the intensively grown shop-sold ones, seem to grow haphazardly, appearing in places not seen before, sometimes singly and sometimes in groups. Occasionally we find ones so large that they only just fit into the frying pan, and cover the whole plate. Fried in butter and accompanied by home-cured bacon they provide a superb meal. The field mushrooms, which are smaller and whiter than horse mushrooms, may start to appear about this time too, and often these grow in places where cattle, sheep or horses have been fed and concentrated the dropping of their manure. These field mushrooms are also delicious, and superior in flavour to those grown artificially. However, the mushrooms are parasitized by tiny flies that lay their eggs either in the soil or in the developing fruiting body, and these hatch rapidly into very small maggots that tunnel their way up the stems of the fungus into the main part, where they eat and grow with speed before the fungus rots. Consequently it is preferable to pick mushrooms early in the morning before these little maggots have attacked the newly-emerged buttons. It has always astonished me the speed at which quite large mushrooms appear. One can pick all visible fruiting bodies – for that is what mushrooms are – one morning and next morning more may have appeared, and later in the day if these are left, quite large open mushrooms can be found. It is fascinating to think of the intricate mycelium that grows beneath the soil which throws up these fruiting bodies to shed spores. These spores can be seen if one leaves a mushroom for a day or so on a white plate. Below it will be found a film of dark powder, which is formed of the millions of tiny spores that would normally be spread by the wind if the fungus was left in the field.

Delicious as mushrooms are, I find that one tires of them after eating them for several days in succession, if we are fortunate enough to find a sufficient crop. On the other hand, I do not tire so quickly of eating chanterelles, and these have the added advantage that they do not get infested with maggots. Occasionally one finds slugs feeding on them underneath, or harvestmen sheltering below them, but these are easily removed. Chanterelles grow in woods, and are symbiotic with certain trees and their root systems, including birch, beech and some fir species. The first appear in July, and they continue to appear in various places in the woods until September. Their abundance is influenced by weather conditions, and mostly they seem to grow well in drier conditions than the humid ones favoured by field and horse mushrooms. So poor mushroom years are often good seasons for chanterelles. Very wet conditions are not much good for either, and chanterelles that have been subjected to a lot of rain tend to go rather slimy and are not worth collecting.

The growth of grass naturally checks in the middle of summer, and at this time of year, especially depending upon the weather, the grazing of the fields has to be managed to achieve a satisfactory level. The removal of rough grass causes the plants to send out fresh shoots, and these are both more attractive to stock and more nutritious. Contrary to what some people might imagine, long grass is neither so attractive nor so beneficial to livestock, and the ideal is to try to maintain grass growth at a few centimetres height. Grass that is allowed to grow too long becomes coarse and cattle and sheep leave it uneaten if there is a choice of sweeter grass. However, cattle will eat longer and coarser grass than sheep, and so use of the two types of livestock in sequence helps to maintain the grass at a suitable height, with the cattle, especially older cows, eating off the older, longer herbage, followed perhaps by younger cattle and then by the sheep. Alternating the grazing of cattle and sheep also has the advantage that most of the internal parasites of one species, such as bowel worms, tend not to affect the other species, and the grazing beasts absorbing the eggs that have been evacuated onto the pasture help to reduce the problem for the host species. Older cattle and sheep tend to develop a degree of immunity to internal worms as well.

It may be that with restricted grazing for cattle, available grass can be maintained at suitable grazing height by the use of beasts of different age groups, allowing younger stock to graze fresher grass first, possibly alternating these with a few sheep, but where most of the sheep flock is run on the hill ground in summer these may be utilized as a change of grazing in the fields when periodically they are brought down briefly for handling for dipping or foot treatment, or for weaning the lambs, and so on. The task of gathering the sheep off the hill may well be such that this takes a day or most of a day on extensive hill, and even on quite small areas when there is a lot of cover in which sheep can disappear, so collecting them into a field ready for handling in the pens on a following day, depending upon weather, may be more convenient. Wet or hot sheep are best not handled, therefore dipping should not take place in wet conditions or when the animals are hot after walking some distance.

Sheep are dipped to rid them of external parasites. These may be tiny mites that cause sheep scab, against which all shepherds had to dip sheep compulsorily for a number of years until recently, when the disease was brought largely under control, or, more commonly sheep are dipped to rid them of, and give them protection from, ticks, lice and flies. In some hill country ticks are a major problem, since not only do they carry disease, such as louping ill, and organisms that cause tick pyaemia in lambs, but their action in sucking the blood of the sheep is itself injurious to robust health, and sickly animals can be further debilitated by high tick burdens. In bad tick areas sheep may have to be dipped at least twice in a season, if not several times, to give them adequate protection. Dipping of sheep is quite an expensive business, since all chemical medicaments are costly, and it is also laborious, for although dipping baths have been designed to facilitate the job, the gap between theoretical and practical operation is usually considerable. Our system involves sheep entering a short race, encouraged by a penned 'decoy' sheep ahead of them, just behind which, is a sloping ramp with the side next to the dipping bath replaced with a curtain. The theory is that the sheep move into the race up to the decoy sheep, slip sideways on the sloping ramp, and fall through the curtain into the dipping bath. In practice the sheep smell the dip and the ewes know perfectly well what is in store and are extremely reluctant to enter the race at all! When they do so, they usually try to back out of it again, and when unable to do so because of a gate closed behind them they stand steadfastly refusing to move forward and so have to be dragged or shoved individually to the ramp, and even then most of them manage to cling to the top of this with their forefeet and resist tumbling into the dipping bath in accordance with the theoretical procedure.

Dipping can be a laborious, and occasionally somewhat traumatic, job, particularly when the farmer is single-handed, and there is constantly the worry of problems arising, even possibly from inhaling the fumes of the organophosphorus dip, let alone from being splashed by the chemical, which seems inevitable despite protective clothing. Recently it has been shown that exposure to the organophosphorus chemicals used in sheep dips can result in debilitating neurological disorders including depression, headaches, sleepiness, lack of co-ordination, loss of memory and pains and numbness in hands and feet. One report indicated that one-third of sheep farmers believed that they were adversely affected by exposure to sheep dip. With these types of problems specific association with the chemicals involved is difficult to prove and further research is currently taking place. Such neurological disorders would be difficult to discern in sheep of course, and one wonders what the actual effect on these animals must be when immersed in the chemicals if the symptoms in the humans that handle them is so problematical. Because of worry about these chemicals I have tried preventing flystrike (the laying of eggs by flies on dirty wool that subsequently hatch into maggots) on the sheep by using alternative spray-on insecticides that have recently become available as a result of the concern over organophosphorus products.

Some ewes will go on milking well into September, and there is some advantage in selling lambs straight off the ewe insofar that weaning tends to set the lambs back some days, for they spend much time yelling for their mothers rather than feeding. However it is also important to ensure that the ewes are in good and rising condition at tupping time, when the rams are introduced into the flock. In order to try to protect ewes against mastitis they need to be dried off as rapidly as possible, perhaps by putting them into an area with little grass for some days to dry up their milk supply by restricting their food. Some farmers favour weaning lambs at twelve to fourteen weeks old, not only to enable ewes to build up their condition again, for ewes giving a lot of milk put the benefit of their food intake into the milk supply rather than their own body condition, but also to put the lambs onto clean fresh grass to ensure the best growth. Thus some farmers may decide to start weaning lambs around the end of July, putting these onto better grass without the competition in feeding from the ewes, and putting the latter back onto poorer hill grazing for a time. However there are many hill farmers that do not have good grazing fields available in which to put lambs, and so they have to remain on the hill grazings with the ewes until sale time.

The stress caused by weaning, and possibly moving lambs onto good grass, can sometimes precipitate problems with pasteurellosis or one of the other diseases to which lambs are prone. Unfortunately the symptoms of these diseases are generally simply finding a lamb, or other sheep, lying dead, and it is particularly distressing to find store lambs, usually the biggest and best ones, lying dead in the field one morning for no obvious reason. The precaution against these diseases, by no means always completely successful, is to vaccinate lambs, which require two doses a month apart. This means two handlings of the sheep specifically to vaccinate the lambs prior to weaning. Lambs that are continually grazed with ewes in fields with good grazing are not quite so susceptible to such problems since they do not encounter the change from poorer hill grazing to lusher grass in the fields, which often precipitates these latent diseases. Nevertheless stress and trauma of any kind have a bad effect upon sheep and continual handling, crushing in pens, changes in feed, and even sharp changes in the weather can trigger off diseases, and farmers have to be continually watchful. Sheep farming is by no means a simple matter of putting sheep onto the hill or into a field and leaving them for the summer and then selling the lambs in the autumn.

August

On hills in the north August is the month when the heather blooms. It is a warm month when many tourists visit the hill country and see the lovely purple of the heather flowers on the high hills, and all seems peaceful. There is not yet the bustle of harvest activity that takes place on low ground farms at this time of year, for harvest comes later on upland and hill farms. Indeed the oat crop, where this is grown, will not be ready for harvesting until October in most years, and I have known a neighbour to harvest his oats on New Year's day in a year where persistent wet weather in autumn denied him the opportunity before. Straw that has lain all winter as a result of wet weather preventing it from being baled has occasionally been secured eventually as late as the following March. Such is the problem of harvest in high country with a short growing season and less amenable weather. August can be a dry month, however, and some of the hill ground is stony and shallow, with light soil and rock not far below. This ground dries out quickly, and fields are apt to burn up in prolonged dry weather. Patches in cereal crops, where hard ground lies close to the surface and the thin soil becomes parched, can wither away, and high points in grass fields burn and turn brown. Grazing can become short in the fields, and in places the higher hill grazing with damp areas can provide better feed than the browned fields. Mostly, in more normal years, the dry period comes at the beginning of the month and sometimes there can be muggy weather at the end, and occasional frosts are by no means unlikely, with clear weather resulting in heavy morning dews.

The grouse shooting season opens on 12 August and we see pictures in the magazines of shirt-sleeved shooters striding the moors. Grouse shooting has taken place on heather-covered hills for two centuries, though in earlier times with the aid of setters and pointers, and even from horseback; driving the birds to waiting guns hidden in butts is a more recent development. In early seasons the heather is in full bloom by then, but in later seasons the purple flowers may only just be starting to appear, or perhaps may not do so until nearer the end of the month. In large areas of the highest hill country grouse shooting and deer stalking are inextricably mixed with sheep farming, and these three uses of the land have formed the countryside as we know it today.

Large tracts of heather moorland exist today, unique in the world, as a direct result of moorland management for grouse for sporting purposes, complemented by sheep farming. On the highest ground, where sparse heather gives way to poor grasses and rock, and grouse are few and far between, perhaps with occasional ptarmigan on the high tops, deer stalking is the primary land use, but in most of such areas this in itself would not be sufficient to justify the livelihood of the inhabitants, and so sheep stocks are carried on the hills as well, with many stalkers and keepers being part-time shepherds, or vice versa. In some parts of the country the heather moorlands are regarded by their owners primarily as grouse moors and managed as such; but on many of these the sheep play a valuable part in grazing heather. The management of grouse depends upon providing the birds with a habitat containing very young heather for their food, and also longer growth for shelter; but avoiding the heather deteriorating into old tough, rank, plants that are useless as a food source and too long for shelter since the grouse may be unable to move properly in its tangle, which also provides better cover for predators. Thus grouse moor keepers burn heather each year in small strips and patches to provide a mosaic of alternating stages of heather growth, since the heather burns only on the surface and regenerates from the roots. This young heather also provides food for both sheep and deer, and reciprocally the grazing by these animals helps maintain some of the heather short, whilst doubtless insects found in the vicinity of their droppings are a valuable part of the food supply of young grouse chicks. The shorter heather areas, and indeed the general

mosaic of differing growth stages of a managed grouse moor provide a suitable habitat for other bird species, and insects too, and the contrast is clear to those familiar with such ground and also with areas of untended, long, rank heather.

By the end of the month the rowan berries are ripening on the trees and already there are the early signs of approaching autumn after the short summer. The small tortoiseshell butterfly, which is one of the few butterflies that overwinters in adult form, seeks shelter for hibernation, and before August has ended we find several of them gathered with wings tightly shut in the dark corners of the woodshed near the ceiling, and in the farm buildings, where they will remain until one warm day in spring when they reawaken, unless some disaster befalls them. One day in winter I was dismayed to find half a dozen pairs of tortoiseshell butterfly wings on the floor of our woodshed. I suspect that a wren, though possibly a robin, since these often come into the back porch of the house, had entered the woodshed and picked off the hibernating butterflies, snipping off and discarding their wings.

The swallows that nest in the farm buildings are joined by others from elsewhere, and together with house martins, perhaps from the distant village, they congregate in growing numbers on the electricity wires. We frequently count well over a hundred perched in rows on the wires. The farm seems to be the annual gathering place of swallows and martins for the area prior to migration. Sand martins, too, from a gravel pit almost two miles away, which we see flying around in small numbers occasionally during the summer, appear in quite large numbers, and a small cloud of them hunts for insects across the fields behind the house and then settles briefly on the electricity wires outside the kitchen window. Then one morning we do not see them again, and the rows of birds perched on the electric wires are all swallows and house martins. These stay for a few more days and then suddenly one morning there are only a few left, the early broods having departed on their way south to warmer climes. The swifts leave earlier still, around the middle of August, but none of these nest on our farm buildings, though we see them from time to time during the summer wheeling and screaming overhead with the swallows. The swifts generally fly high up, more so than the swallows and martins.

Ragwort is a problem on many farms in marginal country. This noxious weed spreads by wind-blown seed, which can lie dormant for a long period, but is very quick to colonize disturbed ground, such as spoil from where ditches have been cleaned out, or even the remains of molehills in the fields. Normally ragwort will not be eaten by cattle or horses, but it contains a poison that accumulates in the liver and can ultimately kill either of these animals if consumed. Wilted ragwort, and indeed thistles, and many other plants, seem to acquire a more attractive taste for herbivores, and so do plants freshly sprayed with herbicide. Cattle will readily eat freshly sprayed thistles if allowed the opportunity, and it is important that stock is removed from any fields in which ragwort has been sprayed until the plants are completely dead and unpalatable. The danger with ragwort lies not so much in the odd beast eating it for some reason, but with plants contained in hay and eaten in error, and more so in silage where the individual plant constituents may not be readily recognizable. Usually cattle will pick out thick stems of thistles, docks and ragwort from hay and discard them, but the leafy parts are easily eaten in a mouthful of grass. It is wise to try to avoid the risk of exposing cattle and horses to ragwort, and especially to ensure that they are not kept in

areas where the plant grows and there is little other food choice so that they might be tempted to nibble the plant when it would normally be ignored.

For some reason sheep are less susceptible to ragwort poisoning, and both sheep and deer will readily eat both the flowers and the plant. After years of spraying ragwort according to advice received from experts and chemical company representatives, including doing so at differing times of the year and doubling, and on one occasion even trebling, the strength of the spray (we do not spray chemicals on the farm now), with little discernible success, and obvious checking of the clover content of the grassland, we resorted to the old-fashioned remedy of using sheep, which has been successful; although the plant is by no means eliminated from the farm, which remains exposed to seeds still in the ground and also blowing in from rough ground and neighbouring heavily infested farms. With small infestations, pulling out the ragwort plants may clear the area, but it is important that the entire root system is removed, since if parts of the plant are left it will regenerate and regrow the following year, changing from annual to biennial. Continual grazing by sheep, especially eating the flower heads, prevents seeding and weakens the plants, and after a period of years a heavy infestation can be reduced to the appearance of only small, scattered, weak plants, and eventually the problem will be reduced to tolerable levels. It is not clearly understood why sheep and deer can readily eat ragwort without apparent harm, but one theory is that the alkaloids that affect the livers of cattle and horses are broken down in the rumen of the sheep. An alternative idea is that there is a difference in the alkaloid metabolism of the livers of sheep. Although it is not certain that sheep are definitely not susceptible to ragwort poisoning – discussion and advice usually carries the warning that there may be risk – we are unaware of problems having occurred with our sheep. However, it is impossible to know always the cause of death of most of the sheep that die on the farm. Moreover, it seems logical to take the view that if sheep readily and spontaneously eat ragwort, with no apparent adverse result, the idea that animals generally distinguish plants that are distasteful or toxic to them is probably correct.

Bracken is another plant that causes great problems on hill farms throughout the country; it is of major economic detriment as well as a health hazard. In August this pernicious weed is at its height. Bracken has the disadvantage of favouring the better ground, and spreading extremely fast; it now covers huge areas of otherwise valuable grazing and increases at an alarming rate. Previously the only treatment against bracken was laboriously cutting by hand or slashing with machinery the emerging fronds at the brittle stage, which had to be continued annually, gradually weakening the plants and their massive under-ground rhizome system. Very heavy temporary stocking, especially with cattle, to trample the emerging fronds, would have the same effect but is mostly impractical. The major problem with bracken is that it covers vast areas with such a thick canopy overhead, and such a thick, expansive, underground rooting system that other plants are unable to grow, except a few weak grasses where light penetrates between bracken clumps or along worn paths. A secondary problem is that bracken provides an ideal environment for ticks, with adequate shade, and herbage against which animals brush, enabling those parasites to scramble onto their hosts for a blood meal. The third problem is that it is now known to be a carcinogen, but it also causes a thiamin deficiency in horses as well as affecting bone marrow function in cattle and sheep.

Although horses will eat some bracken spontaneously, they will have to ingest a significant amount over a period for symptoms to appear and it is advisable to restrict access to the plant. Sheep seem less susceptible to direct bracken poisoning but it is difficult to identify the cause of death in sheep. Cattle and sheep are most likely to eat bracken during periods of drought, when the plant remains comparatively succulent. The symptoms may not occur until a couple of weeks after cattle have been removed from bracken-infested ground. We lost one cow and almost lost another from probable bracken poisoning during the 1976 drought. They had been put on old fields on the hill that had been largely cleared of bracken by spraying by helicopter – the cost substantially grant aided – the previous season. However, some bracken remained in a small area. The ground was very dry, though less so than the fields below, and a tiny stream trickled through a damp area of ground on one side, so perhaps the cows preferred to munch the more succulent bracken than walk across for a drink, though the distance could be no more than a few hundred yards. About a fortnight after the cows were brought down into the fields, where welcome rain had encouraged a little grass regrowth, two cows showed signs of distress, one especially so, and I called the vet. The cows' faeces were dark, showing signs of blood clots; bracken poisoning was diagnosed and the prognosis held out little hope. That evening I saw the worst affected cow suddenly appear to have a fit and drop dead. The other cow recovered.

A chemical spray has been developed that is effective on bracken. This chemical was originally developed for killing deep-rooted weeds such as docks. However, it was found to be successful on bracken; although it also checks many of the hill grasses but these recover the following year, and it may cause some damage to trees. I do not care for the idea of spraying chemicals if this can be avoided, but there is little other method of bracken control that is practically effective and so this was the spray that we chose to apply in 1975 on the bracken-infested part of the hill. At the time of spraying it has no apparent effect, but the bracken simply does not reappear next year. However, any small remaining clumps not touched by the spray have to be resprayed the following year or the bracken will spread again, and often heavy stocking with beasts is necessary to trample any other emerging growth. Failure to ruthlessly destroy any surviving bracken in the area will result in gradual reinfestation and within five years this will be as bad as before. August is the time for spraying bracken, for this has to be done when the fronds are fully grown but undamaged by frost or senescence. Bracken that has suffered from frost, or been damaged in spring, for instance by slashing, will not uptake the chemical sufficiently for satisfactory effect.

Spraying bracken is at best difficult, and at worst impossible. In many areas of hill and rough ground spraying is possible only from the air by helicopter or light aeroplane, which makes the operation extremely expensive, on top of the considerable cost of the spray itself. Even on comparatively smooth ground, without too many rocks, boulders and other obstacles, spraying is difficult, if not dangerous, when carried out with a vehicle-mounted spraying machine, because it is impossible to see clearly where one is driving in the thick foliage. Moreover, in tall bracken the spray booms require to be mounted very high to be above the canopy, and uneven ground can cause these to tilt so that they hit the bracken fronds. On rough ground spraying by vehicle is obviously impossible. The alternative, spraying by hand, is incredibly slow and laborious and practically can be used only in small areas. The result of these difficulties is that many hill farms are faced with bracken areas which they cannot eradicate, and the farmer can only

battle to try to avoid the plants spreading further. Gathering sheep in bracken-infested areas can be very difficult and laborious, for the animals may simply hide in the thick growth and some can easily be missed.

Flies can be extremely tiresome in late summer, especially to sheep; but they can also be responsible for summer mastitis in cattle, many cows losing the use of one or more milking quarters as a result. Whilst sheep seek some protection underneath the bracken canopy, this itself harbours highly irritating small 'bracken flies'. Especially in warm weather, flies can be desperately bothersome to both sheep and cattle. Horned sheep in particular are pestered by head flies, which create sores around the horns and on top of their heads, and once opened up the flies keep these wounds open and make them worse, tormenting the sheep. Treatment by the application of expensive insecticides can help, but is by no means a reliable alleviation, and badly affected sheep may require frequent application to keep the flies away and allow the sores to heal. Flies are adept at locating even tiny sores on animals, and their persistence inevitably opens up and increases the wound, which in turn attracts more flies. Dipping the sheep helps to some extent by giving protection for a period. Small cuts and abrasions can quickly become quite major sores with constant attack by flies, and the farmer has to be watchful, and if necessary catch the sheep or bring them into the pens for treatment.

Flies spread the organisms that cause mastitis and are responsible for this disease in cattle, and even horses, as well as in sheep. Unattended mastitis results in the affected teat and section of the udder swelling up into a hard, inflamed area that causes the animal pain, and may make walking difficult. Usually the course of the disease may not be so dramatic, and the result on the infected quarter is that the internal milk-producing tissue is destroyed; but in extreme cases, more often seen in ewes than cows, since the latter are more easily noticed and more likely to be treated, the udder can burst. This could be fatal, but many ewes recover, despite the trauma of the burst udder apparently exposing a revolting-looking wound to other problems. Either part of the area seems to slough off or it degenerates and shrivels, and the wound recovers to the extent that late in the autumn it may require careful examination to locate the affected ewe for casting from the flock for sale. Mastitis is a major problem with dairy cattle, where clearly the effect on the milking ability of the cow has economic repercussions. In the case of hill suckler cows rearing one calf the loss of the function of one teat may not be disastrous, but the loss of milk in one teat of a ewe is critical, for she will be unable to feed a lamb on that side. If this condition remains undiscovered until next lambing season and the ewe has twins, the result will be either the death of one lamb, should the milk-less teat not be discovered rapidly, or the necessity of that lamb being raised by another ewe or by artificial means.

Mastitis can occur at any stage in female animals. It appears sometimes in heifers before they have given milk and in ewes at lambing time, and not only during the milking period. Indeed we have seen an elderly mare that had not had a foal for fifteen years have one side of her udder swell up with an infection of mastitis, necessitating antibiotic medication.

Thus flies are more than the cause of considerable irritation for animals, but carriers of disease too. Some flies are themselves parasitic on farm livestock, and in particular warble flies and bot flies menace cattle. Signs of their presence are when cattle lift their tails in the air suddenly and rush across the field in apparent panic. The warble fly lays its eggs on the legs of cattle, and these hatch into small maggots that burrow into the skin, and then, over a long period, migrate through the body to finally appear in early spring as large grubs under the skin of the back, from which they eventually emerge. Bot flies have equally unattractive breeding habits, including the nasal bot fly whose maggots thrive in the nasal cavity of the unfortunate victim. Until three years ago I never saw a maggot on our sheep here, even when some lambs were scouring badly in summer. However, this can be a major problem in many parts of the country. Whether as a result of several mild winters, I do not know, but the problem arose in our flock three seasons ago and we discovered several ewes and lambs with bad maggot infestation. The following seasons also produced several flystruck sheep despite the last summer being unusually cold. The surprising observation was that in each of these seasons we had less trouble with flies in the house than in many years previously. The flies seemed to have chosen to pester the sheep instead!

Flystrike is a particularly revolting condition, and can be difficult to detect in early stages. Sometimes the only indication is that a ewe or lamb is clearly itchy or in discomfort, and either continually lying down, or turning its head round to the affected part. Flies may be attracted to a small area of dirty wool, or a small cut or sore. Once a fly has laid its eggs and these have hatched into maggots, which only takes a day or two in warm weather, the feeding maggots produce a horrible smell, which undoubtedly attracts other flies, and the whole affliction becomes compounded. The wool of the maggot-infested area becomes grey and damp, and this is often accentuated by the unfortunate sheep lying on that part to try to relieve the discomfort or prevent the attention of other flies, causing the area to become warmer and damper and a better environment for the maggots. These eat the base of the wool and the skin and flesh of the sheep, in bad cases causing the wool to drop off exposing a raw wound, whilst the maggots migrate to the wool at the side and extend it. If untended the unfortunate sheep will eventually die, distracted by the torment and unable to eat and presumably in pain. Treatment involves clipping away the affected wool, which is usually thick with a seething mass of maggots by the time that the symptoms are noticed, and spraying the area with both insecticide to kill the maggots and deter new infestation, and treating any sores or wounds with antibiotics.

In late August the signs of the annual cycle of myxomatosis and coccidiosis begin to appear in the rabbit population. One sees odd rabbits suffering from myxomatosis occasionally throughout most periods of the year, sometimes even very young rabbits, but mostly this disease appears in late summer and early autumn each year, lasting several weeks or a couple of months before largely disappearing again. Many surviving rabbits show signs of having had the disease and recovered, indicating either a degree of immunity or a weakening in the virus. Most young rabbits have some sign of hepatic coccidiosis, or liver rot, at this time of year, and some of them succumb whilst others recover and develop immunity. It is this disease that effectively controlled the rabbit population from reaching plague levels over the centuries in this country, before myxomatosis was introduced. However glad a farmer may be that these, what might be called natural factors, control the rabbit population to some degree, nevertheless the unfortunate rabbits suffering from myxomatosis, with swollen orifices, the wretched animals being unable to see or hear properly, are a sickening, unpleasant spectacle. Myxomatosis is spread among the rabbits by fleas, which explains why some rabbits lying out on the hill or in cover seem less prone to infection by the disease than those living in burrows. Interestingly it was discovered that the rabbit flea's own breeding cycle is dictated by the rabbit since it only breeds when the rabbits are breeding, being controlled by hormones

in the rabbit's blood. This may have a bearing on the cyclical or seasonal nature of the annual major outbreaks of myxomatosis each year. Most young rabbits show signs of coccidiosis at this time of the year, internally if not externally, unless it has been a particularly dry summer.

All is not disease and disaster in August though. For roe deer the life cycle is restarting, since the rut takes place at this time of year, when mating occurs, and occasionally one catches a glimpse of a roebuck chasing a doe on the hill or through the woods. Roe are not herd animals, like most of the other deer in this country, and so the rut is not an antagonistic affair with males skirmishing with each other, as is the case with red deer, fallow and sika. Warm sultry weather seems to produce greater mating activity amongst the roe. It is just such weather that precipitates the emergence of flying ants too, which provide a feast for many small birds. One day, walking home along the farm track in the gloaming on a sultry August evening I became aware of toads on the road every few yards, in numbers that amazed me. I discovered that they were feasting on the huge numbers of flying ants that had emerged and were walking all over the ground. Although we quite often see a toad on the garden path after dark, and find them when we move large rocks or items that have lain undisturbed for some time, crouched in the shade and cool, I do not recall having seen them in such quantity on any other occasion as on that night. One summer a toad lived in our byre beside where we fed the cat with rabbits. We often saw the toad by the rabbit remains, but did not establish whether it was catching flies or maggots on the carcase, or whether it ate bits of rabbit dropped by the cat, or fed direct from the remains.

The new frogs have emerged from the ponds some time ago, and occasionally we see one in damp ground near the ponds, but mostly we see them rarely except

at spawning time in the spring. It is astonishing to see the enormous numbers of frogs in some of the ponds at that time, and one wonders from whence they have come, and where they live during the remainder of the year. There is undoubtedly a substantial frog population in many damp hill areas, which mostly carry a high population of insects and slugs too. Frogs and toads spend most days sheltering under rocks and in holes or other damp cover, emerging at night to hunt for prey.

Some of the earlier wild fruit harvest ripens in August. The fungi that started appearing in July continue growing in August and one can still gather a few mushrooms in the fields, often on those farms that had horses comparatively recently, whilst in the woods the chanterelles can still be found until the end of the month at least. The wild raspberries are ripe, and though the berries are mostly small, the flavour is greatly superior to those of the cultivated fruit. Most of the wild berries remain ungathered, but are appreciated by many birds. The geans are ripe too, though the crop varies from year to year, and the cherries are very susceptible to being blown off the trees by strong winds before they are fully ripe. These wild cherries again have an excellent flavour, but the proportion of fruit to stone is low, and cherry pies made from geans need to be eaten outside where one can spit out the many stones onto the ground uninhibited, or consumption becomes something of a labour! The blackbirds and thrushes, and many other birds, including rooks, gorge themselves on geans. We often find large pellets, of the size of fox droppings, composed almost entirely of gean stones round the farm, in the fields and on top of gate posts. I might have thought that those on the ground were from foxes, which doubtless favour fruit when given the opportunity, but the pellets on top of posts and so on could not be from foxes and I deduce that rooks are responsible. These birds are also undoubtedly responsible too for dropping fir cones and old empty shotgun cartridge cases in the fields, far from the nearest conifers, and the cartridge cases are of unrecognizable and unknown origin.

The mystery as to why corvids seem to favour coloured objects and pick them up and carry them is fascinating. Perhaps jackdaws, more renowned for their attraction to colourful or shiny objects, are responsible for dropping these objects in the fields rather than the rooks. The behaviour of birds and animals is a fascinating subject, and one in which interest comes rather naturally to many farmers, even if they have no interest in wildlife, for to be competent stockmen and stockwomen they need to observe and be familiar with the behaviour of their animal charges, be these sheep, cattle or poultry. One facet with which most people that look after farm animals are familiar is the racism and sexism in the farmyard.

Where groups of young cattle comprise bullocks and heifers together in the same field, very often these will be seen to be grazing, and especially resting, in groups of the same sex. The bullocks seem to prefer the company of bullocks much of the time, except perhaps when a heifer is bulling, and the heifers seem to

prefer the company of their own sex. The same applies to wild herding animals of course, and apart from at rutting time most deer of the larger species tend to separate into groups of one sex for much of the year. These deer seem to prefer the company of their own gender and come together only for the purpose of procreation. Animals are very conscious of the roles of differing sexes. They are also very aware of ethnic differences too, and one has only to look around a farm with different animal breeds to see how they choose spontaneously to separate from each other. In our farmyard the different species of poultry keep apart, of course, and are often aggressive to each other – for all have complete freedom to wander at will and are not enclosed in any way other than being shut up in sheds at night for their own protection from foxes and weather. The geese tend to be aggressive, especially towards the ducks, or to any hen that is broody or has small chicks. The turkeys tend to stay in a group together, as do the geese, and occasionally when one picks a fight with a Light Sussex or bantam cock they all gang up against him like an evil bunch of mafia bullies. The bantams stay very much in their own groups, and so do the larger hens, and the poultry rarely come together except at feeding time. It is noticeable that different breeds of chickens stay in their own groups and do not integrate, and appear to be aware that they are the same as those of similar breed and different from those of others.

Cattle and sheep also seem to show obvious ethnic awareness, for they have definite preference towards associating with animals of similar breed or colour. We run a mixed flock of sheep, with ewes of three differing breeds, Swaledales, Bleu du Maines, and Mules (which are actually a cross). The Swaledales, which are horned sheep with black faces and white muzzles, longish fleeces, and of hardy hill breed, tend to stay mostly together in loose groups, especially when on the hill. The 'white-faced' sheep tend to be mostly together, though there is some mixing. The blue-faced sheep generally stay in a group too, seeming to prefer the company of their own kind. The hardier hill breeds seem to prefer higher ground, and perhaps rather different choice of food. The tups (rams), which stay in a field near the farm when not with the ewes, certainly appear to prefer the company of their own kind, and the Swaledale tups almost invariably lie a little separate from the others, usually in proximity to each other. Our cattle are a mixture of Herefords, pure-bred and crosses, Blue Greys and Luings. Although there is more integration now that most of the cows have been together for a number of years, and segregation is less noticeable when they are in the fields where they cannot spread out very far, on the hill in winter the groups tend to split somewhat to graze on different areas of the hill, with the Blue Greys, sometimes with a few Luings, tending to feed far from the bunch of red and white cattle during most of the day, all coming together at morning feeding time. Given choice they seem to prefer the company of the same sort of cattle, perhaps having similar preferences for food herbage and conditions.

Both cattle and sheep are highly conscious of strangers: that is not solely humans with whom they are not familiar, but also strangers of their own species introduced to the flock or herd, and even beasts that were once part of the group but subsequently separated for a time and then returned. These are subject to much scrutiny by some of the group, with perhaps their re-establishment in the correct place in the 'pecking order' of the herd, with much jostling and chasing around and occasional fighting. The establishment of a 'pecking order', or social hierarchy, in most animal groups is well documented, and in all of these can be seen 'leaders' that generally come first to feed or lead the group to new pastures. These are usually the dominant animals, that seek and demand the best food and shelter, and the less fortunate ones that are at the bottom of the pecking order are bullied by the others and often too timid and frightened to push in for food at feeding time. The shepherd and stockman will be aware of all these idiosyncrasies amongst the animals in his care and where possible makes provisions to help these less favoured animals.

Sometimes there seems to be a sort of psychological factor involved too, which is more difficult to overcome. At one stage we had three turkey stags. At breeding time these were somewhat aggressive to each other, not surprisingly. However it appeared that the two dominant birds seemed to gang up on the third, and although they did not appear to inflict severe physical damage, it seemed that they had ostracized him and ordered him out of the yard. Some of the cocks, particularly bantam cocks, can be very aggressive and can inflict appalling damage upon vanquished rivals. Once beaten and bloody the victim then tends to be set upon by other birds. Our largest Light Sussex cock was beaten up and usurped by one of his offspring, and moped in a corner of the yard covered in blood from being savagely wounded by pecks and by the spurs of his rival. Whilst in this state for two or three days he was also attacked by a bantam cock a fifth of his size. He recovered in due course and took up his now secondary role at a safe distance from his rival, though still appearing to be favoured by most of his original hens.

The turkey stag that was evicted from the flock, however, did not recover. He retreated from the yard and I discovered him sitting under a bush refusing to come out to eat, or even to go to roost at night. Eventually after a couple of days I picked him up and put him in a pen with plenty of food and water, where he could not be molested by any other bird. However he refused to eat or do anything except sit, and after a few days died. Perhaps he was ill originally and set upon by the others because of this, as birds are wont to do, in pursuance of nature's laws of the survival of the fit and strong.

Currently we have a small cow that is bullied by others in the herd, including animals younger than herself. As a calf she was abandoned by her mother. She was actually born in the field behind the house, because her mother calved very late and it was well into summer. I noticed her trying to suck another cow on her first

day and went to investigate. I discovered that her mother seemed uninterested and would have nothing to do with her. I even got them together into a building, but her mother, who was a heifer, would not let her suck. Her teats were rather warty, and whether they were sore I do not know. We had to bucket feed this calf and rear her ourselves. She became very tame and well fed. Perhaps because she was spoilt, when we introduced her to the herd the other cows and heifers seemed to take a dislike to her, and unfortunately she seemed frightened and would not stand up to them. The result was that she was bullied and ranked lowest in the pecking order. Consequently when the cattle were fed on the hill she tended to get pushed away by the other beasts, and instead of using opportunities to eat she became rather timid. She does settle to eat when the others are all busy eating too, but she was in poorer condition than the other cattle at the end of the winter as a result of being bullied. Unfortunately, presumably also as a consequence of this, she is nervous and no longer tame so that she will no longer take titbits offered to her.

Hill country contains much evidence of ruined dwellings scattered around. It is difficult to know which of the ruins represented houses and which were forms of shelter or pens for animals, though in past times there was not a great deal of differentiation, and at one time the people lived at one end of a building and their beasts at the other end. Often one comes across ruins high up in the hills and these are remains of shielings, where lived the shepherds and cattle drovers who took the herds and flocks up into the hills for summer grazing and stayed there with them until it was time to return to lower ground in the autumn when feeding on the hills deteriorated and the weather worsened. Our own hill is not the high grazing land of the shielings, but there are many ruins of one-time buildings scattered about and I have been told that a large number of families once eked a living on this land.

Around many ruins and derelict farmhouses in this part of the country one can find abundant patches of sweet cicely growing. This tall herb, with a smell like aniseed, is a persistent grower and difficult to eradicate. Often one finds too substantial patches of rhubarb growing around these old dwellings. Sweet cicely is a useful addition to the cooking of fruit as a substitute for sugar in alleviating sourness, and there is no doubt that in the old days, before sugar became widely available and cheap, the herb was used for cooking with the clearly popular rhubarb, and other fruits that were cultivated or gathered from the wild. When it was no longer used and cultivated the plant went wild and grew in profusion untended in the farmyards and outside the garden walls.

Sweet cicely has a white umbelliferous flower, and by this time of year it is starting to seed. The white patches of Queen Anne's lace that border the yard,

giving cover for poultry to nest undetected and emerge later with broods of chicks, and dotted around the edge of one of the old hay meadows, are now seeded too, but in rough corners the rosebay willowherb provides gay patches of pinky-red flowers, much favoured by roe deer in the early stages of growth. On damp patches of ground the attractive melancholy thistle is flowering. It has not got the vicious prickles of its fellows in the thistle family and is quite a welcome adornment. Its name derives from the way that its flowerbuds droop. In the old days the herbalists had the idea of treating like with like, so that they tended to use potions made from the melancholy thistle to cure, or to endeavour to cure, melancholy and depression.

September

September is the month of heavy morning dews, soft mists and mellow fruitfulness; of changing colours of the leaves on the trees and rapidly shortening days, and other reminders of autumn and approaching winter. As the arable farmer gathers in his harvest, and the spring-grown crops come to the end of their cycle, so the hill farmer sees the fruits of his lamb harvest beginning to appear. It is not the end of his sheep year, for he has ahead of him the mating of the ewes and the maintenance throughout the winter months before the next year's lambing, but the lamb crop is only a five to seven month period in the uplands, for the hill farmer is rarely in a position to fatten lambs to slaughter condition and has to sell most of them as stores to be finished by low ground farmers. He may be able to sell some forward lambs direct to the abattoir in September, and perhaps may keep back a few small lambs that would fetch only a derisory price in the mart in the hope of feeding them to sell later in the year at hopefully improved prices, but the bulk of hill lambs have to be sold off when grass growth ceases, the feed value of the grazing deteriorates and lambs will not grow further on the pastures available. Many low ground farmers welcome the opportunity to buy store lambs from the hills not only in the hope that they can add value, and so profit, to these by finishing them with good grazing or turnip feeding to increase their size and weight, but also they value the use of sheep as a tool for managing the grazing of their pastures and improving the fertility of the fields. The conversion of grass and root crops into dung *in situ* increases the fertility of the soil, and many farmers grow root crops as a break in their rotation, utilizing these to fatten sheep. It is this organic method of improving the fertility of farms that earned the name of 'the golden hoof' for sheep in the past.

Sheep can be a valuable tool in grazing management. Grass that goes into winter, with the cold weather and frosts, too long may suffer from 'winter kill', and it is best to graze pastures to a low level before the start of hard weather. Long tufts of grass harbour fungi and diseases that can kill off grass plants in winter. Keeping grass low in autumn also assists the clover content from being shaded out by tall grass. Sheep prefer to graze grass of a lower height than cattle, and so are very useful in trimming fields to a shorter level after cattle have grazed it down. Some lowground arable farmers may not keep grazing livestock for much of the year, but may grow grass as a part of their rotation, or perhaps they may make hay for sale, and lambs thrive on the clean hay aftermath left and make profitable use of the grass field for the remainder of the season. So store lambs may represent an important sideline on farms that do not carry sheep except in autumn and early winter. Hill farms rarely have sufficient arable land to have any available for finishing lambs, and if they have a field of turnips or swedes, these are grown for feeding ewes in winter or at lambing time rather than for fattening lambs.

So, at this time of year the upland farmer has the autumn lamb sales much in mind, for the proceeds of these may represent the bulk of his annual income. Unfortunately there has been a substantial upheaval in the lamb market in recent years, for which politicians and scientists are responsible. A handful of the latter decided to publicize their view that fat was bad for humans to eat, and this was taken up by the supermarket chains with the overwhelming buying power, who insisted that the housewife wanted very lean meat. Now there are signs that this view is changing again and that it is realized that fat is not as bad in a diet as originally suggested. It is also becoming appreciated again, as it was in the past, that fat in meat is required both for satisfactory cooking and for taste, whether one chooses to eat it or not. However the emphasis has for now been put on lean lambs, and farmers have been directed to produce them. At the same time politicians in other European countries decreed that subsidies would be paid on lambs slaughtered, and that these would be targeted to encourage the production of lambs of certain fat levels by paying the subsidy only on those deemed to be neither too thin nor too fat. The fat level was judged by a team of inspectors, and whether a lamb carcase received the subsidy was based upon their personal assessment. As one might expect, personal opinion varied, and three different inspectors might well produce three different opinions on some lambs in a flock; but if a lamb was rejected as too fat or too thin, it could mean that the sum received by the farmer was reduced at times by as much as a third, which could well be the difference between profit and loss. Then the politicians decided, more recently, to abandon these lamb subsidies in favour of alternatives, and this put the lamb market into disarray, with a substantial fall in price per head. This situation has not only had effect on the hill farmers that are the main producers of lambs, but also upon many of the buyers of the store lambs, who hoped to fatten them over the winter.

Without the facilities to retain lambs on the farm, the hill producers lack the flexibility to benefit from rising lamb prices over the winter, and have no option but to sell most at whatever rates prevail in the autumn. The result is that the bulk of hill lambs are sold by producers in a few large sales that take place in September and October. Many of the large sheep sales in various parts of the country take place over several days, with sales for lambs, breeding sheep and cast ewes on separate days. The result of the sale of his lambs may well have significant influence upon a farmer's plans for the following year, based on both the cash realized from the lambs and likely trends, and this will influence his attitude and participation in the subsequent sales of breeding sheep and cast ewes. In 1992 the price for autumn store lambs received by farmers was as low as those that they had obtained for similar lambs in 1978.

September is also a time for the shepherd to sort out his breeding ewes for the following year. Ewes that had problems during the year will have been noted, and probably marked, to ensure that they were were picked out for casting in the autumn. Those ewes that developed mastitis at lambing time, or later, or had been found to have insufficient milk for raising lambs, or damaged teats or other difficulties cannot be used for raising lambs in the future, and so have to be sold and replaced. Similarly those older ewes that have lost teeth and can no longer graze adequately to maintain the required body condition for breeding, especially on hills with a lot of heather or other tough vegetation where a good set of teeth for feeding is vital, have to be cast and replaced since they will not be able to survive hard weather adequately and raise good lambs. There are special autumn sales of cast ewes. Some of the better cast ewes are bought by arable or lower ground farmers with adequate grazing where lack of teeth is of less importance, with a view to putting these to a tup and taking a final lamb crop from them, under more congenial conditions, before they are sold for slaughter. Although undoubtedly buying cast ewes to lamb involves the purchase of a few problem animals amongst these sheep, they represent very cheap ewes for breeding, and they can probably be sold off in better condition for slaughter after a year on good land. Those cast ewes sold for further breeding are allegedly warranted as sound in udder, but at the end of the year it is difficult to be certain of this because the udder retracts so much that only very careful close inspection would detect any problems. The other cast ewes that are not fit for breeding again will go for slaughter and end up as mutton pies or go for export, since there is no market for mutton as butcher meat in this country any more.

The replacement ewes may be bought in, or they may be chosen from homebred lambs. Some farmers prefer to buy strong gimmers (eighteen-month-old sheep, that have been shorn once) from outside to improve their own bloodlines, but most hill farmers probably prefer to use homebred sheep, retaining lambs until breeding age. Apart from this representing a cheaper method of replacing breeding stock, it has the considerable advantage that sheep bred on the farm develop a degree of immunity to some local disease problems, and also they are familiar with the farm as their home ground and become 'hefted' to the hill, and very often to that part of the hill on which they were born, in the case of those lambed on the hill. The retained lambs are called 'hoggs' in Aberdeenshire, though there are many local names for various ages and types of sheep throughout Britain. The hoggs become gimmers after they have been shorn. Although some farmers will put well-grown hoggs to the tup so that they breed from them in their second year, most prefer to have them grow larger first and breed from them as gimmers. Hoggs can present additional lambing problems, both with difficulties in parturition due to their smaller size and to their probably having less milk available for their lamb; and also because, being young, they are sometimes a little difficult about mothering the new-born lamb.

September is the start of harvest time in hill country – long after south country low ground farms have finished theirs. Much depends upon the weather of course, as with the gathering of all crops, and it is not especially unusual for harvest not to be completed on some hill farms until the end of October, and even into November. A friend told me that when she was fishing on the upper part of the river in spring she was watching a farmer baling the last season's straw on the opposite bank. Straw that has lain out in bad weather is of reduced feed value of course, but is still of use as bedding for cattle courts. Barley is an earlier crop than oats and the harvesting of barley crops is finished usually long before the oats are ready to cut. Oats tend to be grown on poorer land with a lower lime content, and so are a more usual crop on hill farms where barley would give poor results. On a very few farms and crofts in the hills oats are still harvested with a binder, and the sheaves stooked to ripen.

Our neighbour used a binder for his oats until a few years ago, building the sheaves into stacks in his yard when ripe and threshing them in a barn threshing machine during the winter to produce both grain and straw for his few cows. His binder was bought new onto the farm by his father in 1905, but later was converted for use by a tractor rather than being horse-drawn, which merely involved altering the drawbar, since the machine is operated by the action of its large wheel upon the ground. Spring-sown oats ripen much later than barley, and by early autumn the weather for crop ripening becomes less frequent. Oats harvested by binder are cut in a greener condition, before they are fully ripe, and perhaps two weeks before the crop would be ready for harvesting by combine harvester. The oats remain in stooks of six or eight sheaves in the field for perhaps a fortnight or longer, depending upon the weather. Sheaves put out by a binder have an uneven bottom with the stalks slightly longer on one side than the other, and they are stacked with the longer side out to shed rain better, with the stook running north to south to give all the sheaves maximum sun for ripening. On most farms that used binders in recent times, especially small crofts without threshing machines, the stooks were fed whole to cattle, to eat both grain and straw in one feed. In past days when fields of stooked oats bordered grouse moors or forests they attracted grouse and black game, and even capercaillie in some areas, as well as woodpigeons. In this area it was quite common on outlying oat fields to see coveys of grouse, or several capercaillie, sitting on top of the stooks raiding the harvested crop.

The harvesting of oats as a 'whole crop' required a considerable amount of labour, for the sheaves had to be collected and stooked, and then the stooks later had to be loaded sheaf by sheaf onto a cart and transported back to the farm and there unloaded and built into a stack. The building of the stack itself required skill. It was usually built upon a base of stones, and often these circular patches of stones can be seen in old stackyards or farmyards. The sheaves are then carefully laid with the cut straw ends out and the grain ends facing inwards in a circular interlocking pattern until the required height is reached, when the top of the stack is gradually sloped inwards to give a weatherproof roof to the structure. With the reduction in available labour resulting from these farms being unable to provide a living for the children of the farmer as well as himself, and the gradual departure altogether of many farmers and country-dwellers to seek a better-paid living elsewhere, these traditional methods of farming necessarily were abandoned. These days the cereal crops are cut by combine harvesters, with the grain transferred to trailers for transport back to the farm, and the straw left in swathes which are quickly swallowed up by big-bale machines.

In autumn the shortening days and frosts or heavy dews at night render the harvesting of late crops more difficult, since it is often well on into the morning before the corn has dried sufficiently for combining to start, and the air

becomes damp again as evening approaches. The baling of damp straw is easier with the large modern machines that wrap it into big, round bales. The old machines that make small square bales are still in operation in a good many places producing bales of more convenient size (the straw is tightly packed before being bound with string), but do not operate satisfactorily with damp straw or hay because the material is too springy. This results in the compacted straw putting too much pressure upon the string and breaking the knots, causing broken bales. As the air becomes damper in the evenings, so does the straw, and this causes the gradual tightening of the bales. The machines that wrap material into big round bales can do so even with green grass, such as is put into bagged silage. However, damp straw or grass causes fermentation and the densely packed material inside the bale produces considerable heat. Although straw tends to give rise to fewer problems with bales heating and going mouldy than with hay, these can still occur with damp straw, especially should this contain a significant quantity of grass from undersowing or weeds. If circumstances allow, often the most satisfactory procedure is to endeavour to bale the straw immediately after combining, when the crop

should be in dry condition, to avoid subsequent deterioration by exposure to inclement weather, or to wind blowing the light straw out of the swathes.

September is a busy harvest gathering time for many animals too, preparing for winter. Hedgehogs can often be seen rustling about in field and wood edges at this time of year, though sadly the sight of a hedgehog is more likely to be a dead one at the roadside for most people. In order to get through the cold winter period in hibernation successfully a hedgehog has to store a food supply in its body in the form of fat reserves, and with the onset of the changing season it is necessary for hedgehogs to eat as much as possible for this purpose before the cold weather arrives. They have to curl up and hibernate in a grass nest in a disused rabbit hole or amongst a pile of leaves, or even in hay bales, until the weather warms up again. Consequently in the autumn hedgehogs become very active in search of food. Young half-grown hedgehogs are particularly vulnerable and most small ones at this time of year are unlikely to survive a hard winter because they will be unable to store sufficient reserves in their still-growing bodies to tide them over the winter. Sometimes they can be seeing hurrying about the fields and woods, and even coming into the farmyard in the middle of the day looking for food, whereas in summertime hedgehogs are mostly crepuscular or nocturnal. On dewy mornings or damp evenings slugs and snails are more active and so easier for hungry hedgehogs to find.

Sometimes on the hill at this time of year we see an occasional red admiral butterfly. These breed on stinging nettle plants, but most of the ones that come to this country in May migrate from Mediterranean countries, where they may overwinter. Some of those bred here seem to try to migrate back to warmer climates and presumably its these odd specimens that we see flying strongly past on occasion. It is amazing to think of tiny butterflies flying across the Channel or the North Sea, but they do so. A friend told me that he was out fishing in his boat at sea, some way off shore, when he observed a butterfly pass him heading out to sea. Migrating too, at the end of September come the wild geese, and at the end of the month we hear and see skein after skein flying high overhead, calling noisily to each other, heading south. Unlike the red admiral butterflies, though, the geese come to Britain to overwinter, on sea coasts or lochs in lowland areas, often in large numbers. The sight and sound of migrating geese heading south is a reminder of winter coming soon. The geese often seem to pass overhead about the time of the equinoctial gales, which occur about the end of September. The equinox, when the day length equals that of the night, occurs on 23 September in the autumn. These gales and leaves blowing from the trees in the wind, are a reminder of the changing season too. The weather, the length of daylight hours and the seasons all influence the farmer's life considerably, dictating his work from day to day and season to season.

The birch leaves start to turn colour at the end of September, and a few yellow leaves spot the ground beneath the trees already, making the last of the chanterelles difficult to pick out among the confusion of colours. The rowan berries are bright red and ripe, and many countrywomen pick these to make rowan jelly. With apples added to make it a little less tart, this is an excellent accompaniment for mutton, lamb or venison. The best berries are those from the trees which it has been noted in previous years are stripped first by the birds, mainly the big flocks of migrating fieldfares and redwings that arrive in this country in November. Berries on some other trees seem to be unattractive to birds. We notice that a holly tree near the farm buildings is invariably stripped of berries by birds shortly before Christmas, whereas two small holly trees on the hill that bear superb bright red berries in thick clusters retain their fruit until the following spring, untouched by birds even in a hard winter. Some hawthorn trees seem to retain their berries too. Most of the rowan berries are eaten eventually, but some trees are stripped of their fruit noticeably more rapidly each year than others.

In hill country in Scotland the last week in September usually heralds the start of the red deer rut. As with sheep, both male and female red deer come into season together in the autumn, and unlike cattle do not breed at other times of the year. During the late winter, spring and summer, the parties of hinds and stags remain separate, generally occupying different territories. However, around the last week in September the older stags start to come into season and the parties of stags break up as the larger beasts wander off in search of hinds. At this time of year stags can be heard roaring in the hills and in some of the woods on higher ground, and in some parts of the Highlands on a still evening at the end of September or in early October the noise of stags roaring at each other can be quite impressive. With the advent of the cooler weather and the disappearance of the grass on high ground the red deer move onto lower ground to feed, especially during the night, and often come into areas frequented by the hill sheep. If the deer come in significant quantities they are not popular with the farmer for eating food that otherwise might be available for his sheep. There is now a growing feeling against red deer, as being responsible for the prevention of the natural regeneration of native woodlands by eating the seedlings, and also for overgrazing heather on which they congregate in large numbers. Very often large herds of deer gather in winter where landowners feed them, and they then stay in this vicinity lured by the free hand-out. The feeding of wild deer usually has little influence upon their antler size or their body weights, in the case of most stags, unless they are fed significant quantities of good quality food. Whereas, encouraging the deer to congregate in numbers is liable to cause the immediate habitat to be polluted by parasites and disease organisms, to the detriment of the

deer. Consequently there is little justification for feeding wild red deer, and having to do so is usually effectively an admission that the local population is too high for the available natural food supply.

In some areas with a high red deer population the damage caused by marauding deer at night to turnip crops can be intolerable, and fencing against such depredations is expensive and not always successful. In the past twenty years the Scottish red deer population has at least doubled. However such a significant increase in deer numbers has also taken place in other countries too over a similar period. Overpopulation can lead to major problems, not just to farmers and landowners, and even to garden owners in some areas, but to the animals themselves. Disturbance and stress, even if caused by their own kind, can affect the deer adversely, as well as enhancing susceptibility to disease, and competition for food and shelter increases with more numbers. In some parts of the country there are undoubtedly too many deer now, and this can be demonstrated by the quality of the animals themselves, which tends to deteriorate as numbers increase, as well as signs of overgrazing in their habitat. However, in some of these areas that are overgrazed the deer alone are by no means responsible, and very often high sheep numbers and unacceptable numbers of rabbits contribute to the situation. Consequently the whole state of affairs has to be looked at properly, and it has to be decided exactly what is required, and whether this requirement is grazing, tree and heather regeneration, or a balance between habitat and animals.

The commercialisation of deer stalking has had an undoubted adverse effect in encouraging large numbers of the animals to be present, both in order that there are plenty available to shoot, and also because deer forests are valued on the basis of the numbers of stags shot, irrespective of quality or weight, there has been an incentive to concentrate upon numbers. In the last twenty or thirty years the tendency to let out stalking, and the lodges for accommodation, and to sell grouse shooting by the week or day, has increased to the point that very few deer forests or grouse moors remain run purely for the sport of the owners and their guests. At the same time forestry has increased substantially since the war, taking the best and most accessible land for planting. This ground, fenced off from the deer, represented not only the best grazing for them, but often also their winter sheltering areas. Likewise it removed sheep grazing ground too. So these animals, often in increased numbers, were confined to smaller areas. Now there is a call from many quarters to reduce deer numbers, and some people are calling for a reduction in sheep numbers too. The problem is that with reduced sheep flocks hill farmers, with incomes already at levels that would not be tolerated by many city dwellers as recompense for their work, are likely to have their farms become completely unviable, and if drastic reductions in deer numbers take place some deer forests will be unable to continue as at present nor will they be able to maintain current staff levels. Such circumstances will inevitably lead to further depopulation of hill country, since the financial 'spin-offs' to local populations from large sporting estates are very significant.

During the daytime the red deer generally retire to the high hill tops where they can benefit from cooler breezes at this time of year to relieve the torment from flies and midges. The Highland midge, *Culicoides impunctatus*, is a major pest in the hills to both beast and man throughout the summer until the reducing daylight hours and colder weather drive them away and kill them. The female midge seeks a blood meal before she lays her eggs in the damp ground, although, if necessary, she can produce these without such a feast. All animals suffer from their attentions, and the hordes of biting midges can often make a shepherd's attempts to handle sheep intolerable, and mostly he will choose cooler or breezy days rather than the still, close ones favoured by midges, to work with the sheep.

October

With the shortening days and cooler weather the growth of grass ceases, and the feed value of grazing diminishes. This means that farmers have to supplement the food available to livestock, especially to cattle, and October sees the commencement of winter feeding. In the autumn the uptake of minerals by plants is reduced, and the small requirement for daily intake of magnesium for cattle may not be met from grazing (and most especially from grazing that has been heavily fertilized), giving rise to the risk of hypomagnesaemia, or staggers. This can be triggered off in particular by stress of any sort, including weather changes, and sharp frosts are likely in hill farm areas in October, and even early snow on the higher ground. As a precaution against staggers, as well as providing supplementary feed, many hill farmers start feeding their cattle cobs containing a magnesium supplement early in the month, or provide the beasts with some hay together with mineral licks or urea blocks containing a high magnesium content. Cow cobs are expensive, but as an insurance or precaution against metabolic disorders the cost has to be compared to the risk of the loss of a beast.

The winter feeding period in what are described in European legislative terms as 'less favoured areas' is a long one, extending probably to over 220 days, which amounts to 60 per cent of the year. The extent of this period, and the shortness of the summers, is probably not appreciated by most people that are uninvolved in hill farming; although those who live in these areas, while not actually farming, but gardening, will be only too aware of the restrictions upon growing many vegetables and flowers owing to the short growing season in hill country and the threat of severe frosts, which occur frequently between September and May, and can occur in any month of the year. Because of the long part of the year during which farmers in the hills have to provide feed to a greater or lesser extent for their livestock, and the limited production capabilities of any arable fields on the farm, their farming policies are largely geared to the provision of winter feed for the maintenance of livestock, which is the main, and in many cases the only, form of economic production possible from hill farms. Whilst some farmers may produce for sale a quantity of grain in the form of barley or oats, in excess of their requirements, these crops are usually grown primarily to produce home feeding material and straw for use on the farm. Hay or silage is made on any suitable in-bye areas, but on many farms sufficient quantity cannot be made and fodder has to be expensively bought, with transport being a significant factor in the cost, as indeed it is in the sale of livestock or produce from the farm which may be many miles from the nearest market. Some of the higher hill farms may have to rely solely upon bought-in feed for their sheep and cattle, where either the fields are too steep or otherwise unsuitable for growing crops, or perhaps there are no in-bye fields at all in wilder parts of the country.

This same shortage or absence of facility for growing home-produced feed for stock dictates that there is no alternative for many of those farmers but to sell the annual crop of lambs and weaned calves in the October sales, leaving only breeding stock on the farm to feed, since there is no capacity for retaining lambs or young cattle over the winter months. Unfortunately this is a time of year when prices for the young stock are low, due to the quantity of lambs and young cattle put on the market by other farmers all in the same predicament. Farmers on low ground, or further south, with grazing still available and fields of root crops grown specially, or large quantities of straw as a by-product on arable farms, and so on, are able to convert this available food into further growth of lambs and store cattle and so profit from this, as well as being able to sell on the animals at a more propitious marketing period – an opportunity not open to hill farmers.

October is the month of the main sales of suckled calves and lambs in most hill areas. In some places these sales are now the only time of year that the local auction mart is used, with the sales activities for the remainder of the year being concentrated in the larger marts in more central areas and large towns. Some of these local autumn sales may handle several thousand lambs and several hundred cattle, and run for several consecutive days, or even a week, with different types of stock being sold on different days. Hopefully these sales are attended by both low ground farmers, butchers and meat traders, and other potential buyers, as well as the consigning local farmers, with the buyers looking to purchase young cattle and lambs to feed on to heavier weights and condition for slaughter, or those beasts that are already in condition good enough for slaughter.

The cheques received from the sale of lambs and weaned calves in the autumn represent the major output receipts of hill farmers, who then have to budget for this money lasting them the whole year until the next autumn sales, with few receipts in between except some subsidy cheques, the timing of which is often uncertain. Consequently poor sale returns mean less cash available for the purchase of bought-in winter feedstuffs. In the recent past low lamb prices have coincided with very high prices for hay and straw, made scarce by poor summer weather, and this combination has meant that making ends meet has become even more of a struggle, if not impossible, for some less fortunate farmers. The introduction of the set-aside policy on cereal growing farms has also contributed to the shortage of straw by reducing the acreage on which cereals are grown, as has the encouragement by generous subsidies to grow oilseed rape and linseed, where such is possible, in place of cereal crops.

When the autumn sales have produced the necessary cash, hill farmers have to think about stocking up with an adequate supply of feed for their beasts for winter. They need to have sufficient stocks on the farm both in case bad weather and snow make access to the farm a problem and the purchase of extra feeding stuff difficult or impossible, and because many of the feeds increase in price throughout the winter. The prudent farmer starts the winter in the knowledge that he has in his barn sufficient hay, straw or silage to enable him to feed his beasts throughout the winter, including the possibility of having to provide extra feed in severe conditions.

On some hill farms there is a degree of shelter in the form of woods or birch scrub on the lower parts of the farm, and in those cases the cattle are likely to be outwintered. Many of the indigenous breeds of cattle such as Herefords and their crosses, Galloways and Blue-Greys, Luings and Highland cattle, are hardy and grow long winter coats giving adequate protection against cold, provided that they have sufficient to eat, and these cattle thrive best out in the open rather than in enclosed buildings. Indeed research has shown that cattle kept in buildings require substantial ventilation as a precaution against diseases such as pneumonia, and animals kept in close proximity to each other are more likely to suffer from illnesses. Nevertheless, on some hill farms in exposed areas there may be little shelter available and the susceptibility of the ground to poaching may render it necessary to house some cattle for the winter where there are buildings available. Cold winds, especially when accompanied by rain, quickly take condition off cattle and sheep that are well able to withstand cold, frosts and even snow. The ability of a hill farm to carry cows thus may depend upon the availability of some suitable shelter for them in hard weather.

Towards the end of October the sheep farmer will be thinking of ensuring that his tups are in good condition, for he will be putting these in with the ewes in November. This may involve a little extra feeding if grazing is in short supply, and ensuring that their feet are in good order. Lame tups are not able to work properly. He will also be sorting out his ewes for breeding and deciding which to cast from the flock and sell if he has not done so already in September. In rough country good teeth are vital for a sheep, to enable her both to crop the sweet short grass that will be in limited supply, and also to enable her to bite through the tough stems of heather and other plants. Old ewes that have lost their teeth can lose condition readily in a bad winter, and will be unlikely to produce a lamb, even if they survive. So it may be better to sell these cast ewes whilst they still have some value, even if that is small. Some years ago an Edinburgh dentist produced a type of false teeth for sheep to try to extend their useful lives, but the idea never caught on successfully. The sheep had to have a plate fitted before the teeth were lost, and this helped to retain them. However, the trouble and expense involved did not justify the exercise, except perhaps in the case of some expensive pedigree sheep, which would probably be fed high quality soft food anyway. Ewes prone to foot trouble are also vulnerable to adverse weather conditions, since they tend to feed less, lying about to avoid standing on sore feet, and so they lose condition. The shepherd can do a certain amount to help these sheep by paring their hooves and treating infected parts, and sometimes making the sheep stand for several minutes in baths of formalin or copper sulphate helps by hardening their feet somewhat. An injection is available to help immunize sheep against foot troubles, but we have never found this very effective. Trimming the feet of sheep from a large flock, where a number of the animals have foot rot, is a very tiring job, with the shepherd having to bend over to clip and pare the hooves and apply antibiotic spray, holding the struggling beast sitting on its backside between his legs.

October is the main period of the red deer breeding season, and from the end of September until towards the end of October the roaring of rutting red deer stags can be heard in much of the Scottish Highland hill country, especially on still frosty evenings. The deer change into their winter coats at this time of year, with the red deer becoming darker grey, with light fawn coloured rump patches extending to over the top of their tails, whilst the roe change from their summer foxy red coats into sleek dark grey with white throat patches and bright white rump patches, which are flared when the animals are alarmed. The hairs of the winter coat of deer are thicker and hollow, giving greater insulation for the protection of the animal in cold and wet conditions. In some parts of the country marauding deer can be a problem for farmers, since stock fences are no barrier, because they can easily jump over them. However electric fences have been found to be a successful deterrent against all deer species, if properly erected, and with the aid of these and a little effort farmers can protect fields of turnips or other crops in this way. The electric fence has to be kept operating efficiently, for deer, like other animals, seem able to detect when the fence is not operating. I suspect that their wet noses facilitate this by sensing a slight impulse at a distance sufficient for them not to actually receive a shock. Care has to be taken that the electric fence does not short and become ineffective, perhaps as a result of wind blowing a branch onto it, or the wire touching other fencing wire, or through snow cover, and so on.

Myxomatosis takes its annual toll of rabbits through most of October in what has now become an annual pattern over the past forty years. The high population of buzzards in many areas, augmented by the now free-flying current year's young birds, perhaps attracted by the rabbits, becomes a familiar sight on many farms in the autumn. We often see three or four buzzards soaring and calling overhead, and have watched as many as ten of these birds together circling and wheeling high above us. Whether the buzzards are attracted by the evident dead and dying rabbits in late autumn in the open

fields, or whether the increase in their presence is as a result of a general movement of the population as the young birds become more independent, I do not know. A couple of times we have watched a rough-legged buzzard on the farm, an occasional visitor from the continent to the east coast, distinguished from the common buzzard by its lighter colour underneath and its feathered legs, and also its tendency to hover more frequently. Although buzzards are unlikely to attack most birds, hawks of any kind cause alarm amongst other species, and so we often see buzzards being mobbed by rooks and crows, and I have watched one being attacked by a heron, and even by a woodcock that repeatedly dive-bombed the buzzard which was flying along the burn side one evening. Buzzards are largely beneficial birds that feed upon rabbits, small rodents and insects, and carrion, although I am uneasy when they are near the farmyard when our poultry have young chicks, and they can cause havoc amongst reared game bird poults. In late winter buzzards spend a great deal of time standing about in fields and on open hill areas catching worms and other small creatures and they do not exist entirely upon large prey or carrion.

Two birds that are familiar to many hill farmers in wilder country, who see them as they walk round gathering or checking sheep, are the somewhat similar

ouzels. The dipper is a charming, smallish, black bird, with a perked-up tail and a prominent white chest with a chestnut patch below. It gets its name from its very obvious habit of continuous dipping movements, bobbing up and down on rocks or stones in streams. Its flight is rapid, usually just above the surface of the water. The dipper lives primarily on water insects, and the bird can swim well under water, feeding below the surface amongst the stones on the bottom of fast-flowing streams and rivers. Although it is smaller and a slightly different shape to a blackbird, the dipper is sometimes known as a 'water blackbird', and also as a water ouzel.

Higher on the hill, in rocky country and wild moorland, lives the ring ouzel, also known by some people as the 'mountain blackbird'. This slightly secretive bird is very similar to an ordinary garden blackbird in appearance except that it has a large white crescent on its chest. Like the common blackbird, which has the vernacular name of 'ouzel cock' in some places, it is also a member of the thrush family. Ring ouzels tend to favour rocky gullies or hillsides near streams, and often one's attention is drawn to the bird by its blackbird-like scolding alarm note: a loud sort of clicking noise.

October often sees the first coverings of snow on the high hill tops, though the first sprinklings usually do not last for long. They are a reminder of the changing seasons and of harder weather to come for those whose lives are closely involved with the hills. At this time of year the days are shortening rapidly, whilst the nights grow longer, and it gets progressively darker in the morning when one rises, and darker earlier each evening. This is a month of more regular frosts, but there can be some glorious clear, but cold, sunny days. On still frosty mornings the ash leaves, by now a lovely pale shade of green, drop steadily from the trees in a silent shower. These fallen ash leaves are a favourite with many animals. Both cattle and sheep let into a fresh field that has an ash tree in it or overlooking it, will hurry straight away to forage for fallen leaves. Many fallen leaves are readily eaten by stock, but ash seems to be the favourite. Similarly ash is favoured by horses and deer as both fresh and fallen leaves.

November

November is a month of preparation for winter on hill farms, and also tupping time, or the breeding season for the ewe flock. Tups, or rams, turned in amongst the ewes at the beginning of November will mean that those sheep successfully served straight away will start to lamb about the end of March. Farmers on lower ground and with in-bye arable fields may start to lamb their ewes this early, in the expectation that grass will start to show the earliest signs of growth at about the time that the young lambs are best able to make full use of the spring growth but those on higher ground, where grass growth starts later and where severe weather often occurs until well into April, may not put their tups in with their ewes until at least mid-November.

On lower ground, where there may still be some grass growth in October, stubbles or other grazing still available upon which to flush the ewes, farmers have this benefit of being able to 'flush', or increase the condition of, the ewes

with existing grazing; sheep in rising condition are more likely to conceive and to shed more eggs for fertilization and thus produce more lambs. In high country, where the grass has stopped growing at this time and no longer has good feeding value, flushing the ewes is achieved only by supplemental feeding with bought-in feedstuffs, and this is both expensive and possibly uneconomical. Moreover, the ewes may well not be in good enough condition after a hard winter and difficult spring to produce a high milk supply and thus unable to rear multiple lambs. Consequently trying to achieve a high lambing percentage in hill country may be unwise and put ewes to heavy strain leading to high lamb losses. Thus, whilst low ground farmers may regularly achieve lambing percentages of 200 per cent, and even more with large numbers of ewes producing triplets, and most expected to produce and rear twin lambs, in hill country the best expectation might be 100 per cent lambing percentage, or one lamb reared per ewe, whilst in much high country it may be difficult to achieve a percentage of lambs reared of much more than 75 per cent, as a result of limited available food supply and poor prevailing weather conditions. Flushing ewes to increase fertility may have little useful purpose under such circumstances.

Ewes come into season in the autumn every three weeks. Although a few farmers having introduced the tups into the ewes will leave them in the flock for much of the winter, most shepherds will prefer a more tightly controlled lambing period. In this case they may leave the tups with the ewes for six weeks, or two complete cycles. By smearing the chests of the tups with marking paint, or putting on a harness holding a coloured crayon on their chests, the back ends of the ewes can be colour marked when mounted by the tup, indicating that service has taken place. This gives a helpful guide not only as to when lambing might be expected to take place, but also as to which ewes might have been served unsuccessfully in the first cycle and re-served later (if the colour carried by the tup is changed after three weeks), as well as those that have been served but have not produced a lamb for some reason. As with most animals, the specific dates for lambing, even with a known date of service, may vary by a few days, and we have found that a ewe can often lamb up to a week at least earlier or later than the alleged due date. Nevertheless, most ewes lamb roughly around the due date, and this gives a useful guide to the shepherd. Sometimes he may wish to know which ewes have been served by particular tups, and in that case may use different colours for marking. Where there are fields available, with sufficient grazing for the sheep over the tupping period, keeping the flock confined facilitates the tups finding the ewes in season and ready for service, but those farms in difficult hill country have to turn out their tups onto the hill to search for the ewes and hope that these are all located satisfactorily. Such tupping on open ground will necessitate the use of rather more tups in proportion to ewe numbers to ensure that the ewes in season are located in time. Where tups are left with the ewes for long periods there is a risk of late lambing from a ewe or hogg (a female sheep in its first winter) having come into season and been served and conceived late, but mostly both sexes will cease their breeding activity by early winter. A few ewes might come into season as early as late September, but mostly they do so in October and November, with the hardier hill breeds doing so later in this period, and younger sheep later still. This coming into season later by hill sheep is doubtless designed by nature so that their lambs are born in kinder weather and when more food is available for the milking ewe.

Different farmers will have differing opinions, and circumstances will vary also, but as a rough guide a mature tup should be expected to serve forty ewes in a field, although he might be capable of serving as many as eighty, whereas a tup lamb might be expected to serve about twenty female sheep. Much will depend upon the total number of the flock and the situation. In hill country the number of tups required will be greater if the ewes are spread over a larger area and thus are more difficult for the tups to find. Some shepherds prefer to use tup lambs when mating sheep on lower ground farms, perhaps with a view to selling on these tups as gimmers (sheep that have been shorn once) the following year, but others prefer older tups, and especially on rougher ground the larger and stronger gimmers will be more active and preferable, with their ability to serve more sheep. After several weeks with the ewes, with their activities concentrated more on procreation than upon feeding, the tups will lose condition and may require extra feeding to recoup this. A fit healthy tup is vital to the productivity of a sheep flock.

There is never a shortage of jobs on a farm, and small maintenance jobs requiring attention are forever present, from greasing and servicing the tractor regularly, mending machinery and repairing fences, to replacing slates blown off steading roofs in a gale and gathering firewood for a winter supply if there is any

available. On many hill farms there may be scrub birch trees that are not especially long lived so there will be occasional dead trees to be removed if in accessible places, or trees and branches blown down by high winds. Birch is an excellent firewood and has the advantage of being a good fuel even when burned green, its difference in moisture content between green wood and dried being smaller than that of most other woods. Ideally it should be dried for some months before burning to produce the most satisfactory firewood, but very dry birch can burn too fast and almost be too hot on occasion. Rowan, when dried, or logs from dead trees, also burns well and slowly, but gives out less heat than birch. Rowan trees are often killed by rabbits and also sheep (and horses) chewing the bark around the base in hard weather when other food is covered by snow and ice and not available. Where the removal of the bark in this way completely encircles the tree it will be killed. Ash wood burns well, and leaves a great deal of very fine ash when burnt. It too burns reasonably well when green, though it is better when the logs have been dried out for several weeks. The wood from conifers is unsatisfactory for open fires because the logs spit out sparks, and it has to be very dry before use. It is better for use in closed stoves.

Unfortunately many animals are fond of stripping bark from mature trees and rabbits are not alone in this. Rabbits tend only to eat the bark from saplings and especially newly-planted trees, except in very hard weather when all is frozen or snow covered when they will strip the bark from rather larger birch and even fully mature rowan trees, aspens and willows. Deer will strip the bark from various trees and in forestry plantations lodgepole pine seem particularly vulnerable. Cattle will chew the bark from some trees but horses can be especially destructive by stripping large areas of bark, especially from rowans, aspens and willows. It may be that these animals obtain some benefit from the bark from some of these trees, rather than stripping them for something to do in a mischievous way. It was noticed long ago that animals often seemed to chew willow when sick, and these observations led to the discovery of its medicinal properties, which in turn led to the production of ubiquitous aspirin. Willow is a member of the *Salix* family, and salicylic acid is the basis of aspirin. Cattle will eat the twigs from lower branches that they are able to reach, from most trees. My cattle know the sound of my chainsaw and in winter will come running to see whether there are twigs to eat if they hear me using it on their part of the hill. They seem to be very fond of birch, which may well contain a high content of some minerals. The younger cattle will actually leave good quality hay to eat freshly cut birch twigs and they eat all of these that they can reach on felled branches up to about finger thickness.

One benefit of the daily feeding of cattle is that they become used to being called to come to the feed and to the sight of feed bags. This can be of great assistance, especially to a single-handed farmer, when he needs to move them between fields, or to bring them in off the hill for some reason, to examine or treat one of them, for example, or to assemble them for the regular cattle test. The test for brucellosis used to be an annual one for many years, but with the widespread eradication of this disease over the past twenty years, with most herds never having a reactor, the brucellosis tests have now been reduced to biennial events. In twenty years we have never had a cow that reacted positively to the tests. Although appreciating the necessity of eradicating the disease, the annual test involved farmers in a great deal of work without recompense. The vet who carries out the tests is paid a fee by the government, but the farmer is under compulsion to present all his breeding cattle for the vet to take blood samples to be sent to the Department of Agriculture laboratories. The blood samples are usually taken from a vein in the animal's neck by inserting a needle attached to a vacuum-filled tube that accumulates the blood. In the case of bulls which not only have thick necks but may be difficult to restrain, or even dangerous, the sample is usually taken from a blood vessel underneath the base of the tail. This procedure often appears to have no traumatic effect upon the bull, which seems to be more concerned by the restraint in the crush or race in which he is held than by the prick of the needle. In the case of a couple of our Hereford bulls it was necessary only for them to stand in the race, and having put a bucket containing feed in front of them we were able to lift their tails and take the blood sample without any sign that they noticed the operation as they happily ate their grub.

The procedure with the cows and heifers for taking blood samples is to move these up a narrow penned-in 'race' or passageway into a 'crush' with a gate holding a yoke. When the cow puts her head through the end gate to try to exit from the race a metal bar is moved across her neck preventing her from withdrawing her head, and with this firmly held a second bar is closed behind her to stop her trying to back. The farmer, or person restraining the beast for the vet, then has to firmly hold the cow's head which is projecting from the crush, and turn this to one side to present the bent neck to the vet so that he can insert the needle into the vein. The cow's usual reaction is to bellow and try to shake her head violently in fear rather than pain, and it can be very difficult holding still the head of a strong, protesting cow and often it requires some strength to do so. All the ear-tag numbers of the cattle, with their ages, have to be recorded. This procedure, involving all breeding cattle on the farm, can be a laborious excercise for the farmer, together with all the work and planning of getting the cattle into pens or a building in the first place; and as the test is compulsory but has sometimes revealed no reacting beast over many years and therefore can seem to be unnecessary work, it can also be a considerable aggravation. For many hill farms this may be the only time in the year that the cows are handled, so that they are unused, and thus reluctant, to enter buildings or pens.

With the leaves falling from the trees and the lovely autumnal colours of October gone, the berries and fruits become more obvious. The rowans, or mountain ash trees, carry clusters of orange-red berries in great quantity, and the hips, or fruits of the wild roses and the haws on the hawthorns add differing darker shades of red to the countryside. In some wooded areas whitebeam berries, and clusters of elderberry fruits are evident. In the north the red-berried variety of elder is often more common than the black-berried species of further south. However, early frosts often damage these berries and the succulent bird food that they represent. Blackbirds and thrushes, amongst other birds, are fond of berries and seem to favour some trees more than others. Some animals like rowan berries too. Foxes favour the geans, or wild cherries, that ripen in the summer, and the gean stones or seeds can be seen in their droppings at that time of year as they can in pellets dropped by rooks, or deposited on the top of fence posts. Rowan skins can also be detected in droppings or on the ground below trees, and in those parts of the country where pine martens are not uncommon, in the north and west of Scotland, their droppings at this time of year can be seen to contain significant quantities of the remains of rowan berries. Rowan trees were thought by many to be a sort of good luck charm, in the old days keeping away witches and evil spirits; so frequently a rowan tree is found growing close to the hill farmhouses and crofts.

The heavy grazing pressure upon hill land by cattle, sheep, deer and rabbits, has meant that in many places the natural regeneration of trees has been curtailed. This can readily be seen from the way that tree seedlings have grown in places inaccessible to these hungry mouths. Many islands in lochs and lakes have trees flourishing on them, and along the banks of streams and burns trees have been able to grow on steep sides where the young plants and shoots cannot be reached by browsers. Similarly in rocky gullies on steep hillsides and on some cliff faces where there is a little soil, tree seedlings have been able to find a protected foothold. Thus, often small rowan, birch or holly trees are found growing in gullies gouged out by burns, providing shelter and nesting sites for birds such as ring ouzels and others that inhabit this territory. The problem of the browsing of seedlings preventing woodland regeneration presents a dilemma to the conservation-minded farmer interested in the countryside and wildlife and favouring natural woodlands, for he has to make a living from the land too, and is unable to do so in hill country without grazing livestock. Moreover, some grazing is beneficial to most of the environment. The problem arises only with the degree of grazing pressure, and this has had to be increased steadily over the years to maintain farm viability in the face of static and falling wool prices and poor returns from lambs. With subsidies paid as headage payments on breeding cows and ewes the incentive has been to increase the size of herds and flocks. Without the farmers in the hills the land would become derelict, and undoubtedly change for the worse, and few people would welcome this or the further depopulation of the hills and the knock-on effects in the whole area. Clearly the ideal would be if the farmers in the hills were able to make a satisfactory living with low stocking rates of cattle and sheep, together with a reduction in deer and rabbit numbers in those areas where these are deemed to be excessive and detrimental to the natural countryside.

The reality of this idea is gradually becoming apparent to those interested in the environment of the countryside, and to those bureaucrats that control the livelihoods of farmers through manipulation of their markets and payment of their subsidies. There is a dawning realization that hill country is stock rearing country, and attempts to encourage farmers to intensify production either by increasing numbers of cattle and sheep and feeding these to later stages of growth, and converting hill grazings into heavily fertilized reseeded grassland, or to drain bogs and wetland and so on, through the exhortations of the advisory services and the offers of grants and subsidies, has had a significantly deleterious effect upon both the countryside and upon the production surpluses, and indeed upon the hill farms themselves. Many farmers must be bewildered by having been encouraged to intensify in the past and yet now find that they are being encouraged to farm extensively in the traditional method, by the same advisers! Agricultural advisers and government officials, who deprecated many conservation ideas only three years or four years ago and advocated heavy use of fertilizers and sprays, and the intensive feeding and rearing of livestock, now find themselves advocating the creation of ponds, the maintenance of bogs, un-ploughed headlands and field edges for the benefit of wildflowers and wildlife, the planting of trees in fields, and the extensification of livestock systems. Some people now see a return to more traditional and low-cost, sustainable farm practices as a desirable way of maintaining, and even restoring, the countryside in an age where this is being appreciated and valued more and more. In times past, when the the population of the countryside was far larger in proportion to the numbers living in urban areas, many more people living in towns had relations or friends or other connections with country dwellers, as in the case with much of continental Europe still. Townspeople had a greater affinity for and understanding of the countryside then. As the population of urban areas swelled and that of the countryside diminished, so the connections between the two lessened. However, more recently there has been a resurgence of interest generated both by a few townsfolk moving back out to live in the country and by increased mobility enabling people to see the countryside and holiday there.

Despite the merit in the call to save and improve the countryside and the scenery in the hills, it must be realized that the hill land has actually been farmed in some degree for centuries and what people now see is the result of farming and shepherding; but the farmers, shepherds and others who live permanently in the hills can continue to do so only if they can derive an income from them. The vision of hills clothed in natural woodland is often apparently misplaced. Much of what appears to be natural woodland derives its attractive open nature as a result of a degree of grazing as well, and some apparent natural woodland is actually man-made. An example is a local National Nature Reserve, created as a result of being designated one of the last remaining areas of natural oak woods in the area. Some years later research discovered that it was not natural at all but had been planted by an earlier estate owner with trees derived from foreign seed! Not far away another National Nature Reserve was created and grazing beasts removed from a large area. The result has been a conversion from heather moorland, and heathland that once contained black game, into thick birch scrub.

The hills are the workplace of those that live there and derive their income from that land, and most of them have a deep attachment to it. Those that seek to use the hills as an opportunity for brief recreation or temporary interest, for holidays or weekends, as the whim takes them, must understand that others have to live there every day of the year, and respect this.

December

With the days growing rapidly shorter the weather in the hills becomes progressively colder, for even in fine weather the sun is low and the daylight is not sufficiently long to warm up the ground. Frosts are normal at night, and snow starts to lie permanently for the remainder of the winter on the tops of the highest ground. On clear, still nights the panorama of the sky dotted with a million stars is sometimes spectacularly lit by the strange searchlight shafts of the aurora borealis, the northern lights. We see these from time to time in the north and the west, resembling the headlights of distant motor cars coming over the hill, only we know that there is no road there, and anyway often they spread over a wide section of the northern horizon. Sometimes the lights are more

from the north-west, and occasionally the flashing shafts are vividly tinged with red or green, continually moving and changing. The northern lights, which are seen most often in the more northern parts of the country, were once thought to be caused by the reflections from polar ice but are now thought to result from 'electric storms' in the atmosphere produced by electrons and protons from the sun, which disturb the atmospheric oxygen and nitrogen causing light to be emitted. These solar particles enter the atmosphere at immense speed, usually in the ionosphere at heights of a hundred miles or so above us, but sometimes much higher. An impressive display of the aurora borealis is the most spectacular and awesome of the heavenly phenomena.

At this time of year we often hear a tawny owl calling in the large ash tree that stands in front of the house at the edge of the farmyard. Sometimes we hear a dog fox barking on the hill too, and we think of the poultry and next season's lambs when we hear him too close to the farm. After the turn of the year we may hear a vixen screaming as well, for that is the time that foxes search for mates. Often we pause in the yard at dusk, when shutting the hens in their shed at night, to watch a party of mallard flighting into the pond on the hill above the farm, once the dam that supplied the water power to drive the corn mill in days past; we see also occasional solitary woodcock flighting overhead in the gloaming on their way from their daytime shelter in the patches of bracken on the hill to the field behind the steading to search for worms and other insects amongst the cowpats. Although a few woodcock nest in parts of the country with suitable cover and woods and stay here all year round, most of them migrate to this country for the winter from colder northern Europe. If we have occasion to go into fields or lower parts of the hill at night with a powerful spotlight to check on a calving cow or some of the ewes, we often disturb woodcock feeding which flutter up in the beam of the lamp. December is usually the month of the arrival of most winter migrant woodcock, fleeing from the colder climes of northern continental Europe; although this depends both upon the weather here and elsewhere. If it is hard weather here the woodcock may move on to the warmer west coast or further south.

When the fields are not frozen or snow-covered we often watch a heron, and sometimes two or three of them, standing motionless or stalking slowly about, in the field in front of the house, on the outlook for worms and insects. Herons do not exist solely upon fish or eels but have a varied diet, including mice, moles and frogs, as well as many kinds of insects and water creatures. Often we see a buzzard there too, looking ungainly as it runs a few steps to peck at the ground on its huge feet, not designed for walking, and giving the appearance that the bird is wearing oversized galoshes or snowshoes. With the supply of sick rabbits succumbing to myxomatosis now no longer present the buzzard must have a harder time acquiring sufficient food, but hunting for worms and insects seems a laborious way for such a large bird to gain a satisfactory meal. However, a buzzard

standing about in a field is a common sight in winter and we see one and
sometimes two almost daily, for much of the late winter when there is no snow or
ice covering the ground. They stand motionless except for moving their heads
about watching and looking, and perhaps listening, and then suddenly they will
run forward a few yards and peck at the ground, sometimes picking up a worm,
or some other food item. Many people think that these large raptors feed only on
quite large animals and birds, and believe that largish mammals like foxes feed
primarily upon rabbits and large birds like pheasants and grouse. However, the
fact is that most of these predators are necessarily opportunists, and whilst they
will all eat rabbits if they can catch them, or indeed pheasants and ducks and so
on, their staple diet is generally a multitude of small creatures and food items.
Buzzards will catch small mammals and eat carrion when opportunity arises, but
they also eat a great many small insects, worms and other small creatures. The
principal food of foxes in many parts of the country and especially in hill country
where alternatives may not be abundant, consists of voles and mice, as well as
berries in season, and even slugs and other small creatures. People that feed foxes
in towns find that as well as items such as eggs and cheese, they are partial to
peanuts, which gives an indication of their widely varied and opportunistic diet.

   The sheep and cattle have now all been put out on the hill, the cattle staying
lower down in the shelter of patches of birch scrub, and coming down to near the

farm road each morning for their daily ration of cobs. If the weather is hard with snow or cold rain or ice, they may start to receive a daily ration of hay too as a supplement to the rough grazing that is still on the hill but will soon be gone as winter progresses. Once the feeding of hay starts it has to be maintained, so, depending upon the amount available as the winter's supply, the farmer will probably try to defer using it as long as there is alternative roughage available for the stock, to ensure that he has plenty to give them in bad weather and when the availablity of the foggage has disappeared. The sheep will not receive additional feed until much nearer lambing time, for they are able to utilize the body reserves built up in summer and at the time of flushing to supplement their diet of hill grazing, unless the weather turns really bad. Even in snow conditions many of the sheep will ignore hay put out for them and prefer to scrape away for fresh herbage on the hill. Salt licks and mineral or urea blocks are provided for most cattle and sheep on the hill, put out in containers and available on an ad lib basis for them to help themselves, to supplement the food that they can pick on the hill with extra minerals and protein.

As the weather gets colder and stormier flocks of redwings and fieldfares arrive from Scandinavia, and can be seen wheeling about over the lower ground where there are trees, and especially rowans, or settling briefly on the grass fields, hopping about searching for insects or seeds, before moving on. For a few weeks there appear to be large flocks of these thrushes constantly flying about restlessly throughout the area, settling briefly to hop about on a grass field for a few

minutes, or settling in the trees for a short time, before being on the wing again. Over the short period of their visit the rowans are stripped of their berries, starting with the apparently sweeter crops of certain trees first and finally the others, until all the berries are gone, leaving traces of orange berry skins on the ground in the vicinity. Hawthorn berries appear not to attract these birds, or perhaps the haws in our area are unattractive to birds for some reason, for these stay on the trees throughout the winter, even in hard weather. Sparrowhawks, which have grown numerous since they were afforded protection as a result of the decline in their population some twenty years and more ago due to pesticides that were subsequently banned from use, are seen quite often and we find the evidence of their taking fieldfares in the form of a few feathers and perhaps the remains of a few freshly cleaned bones. From time to time we find woodcock feathers too, or the remains of a carcase, where a sparrowhawk has made a kill or feasted upon one. Dusk is a time when sparrowhawks can often be seen gliding rapidly low over the farmyard, or twisting through the birch trees with impressive navigating ability, doubtless on the lookout for late-roosting robins or blackbirds, or for woodcock setting out to feed in the fields. The female sparrowhawk is considerably larger than the male. Sparrowhawks are also all too frequent visitors to bird tables in gardens in country districts in winter, and regularly raid the convenient food supply of little birds attracted by peanuts, scraps and seeds provided by householders. To help avoid or alleviate the predation of these small birds from outside the house windows, it is wise to ensure cover for them in

the form of shrubs and bushes, or small trees with thick foliage close to the bird table, into which they can retreat when danger threatens.

In remote hill areas with few trees or other forms of cover, small garden birds may be scarce, but much can be done to encourage their presence by the planting of trees and shrubs around the house. Many farms in these wilder areas have a few trees or a shelter belt planted as a windbreak for the house. Small birds require shelter too, not only for their own comfort, but for all the insects and other food items that it provides. Where bushes have been planted and allowed to grow into cover there will be a noticeable increase in bird life, and watching birds feeding on a bird table can be an endless source of fascination. Some of the birds that frequent the farmyard do not visit bird tables or food put out in the garden. Flocks of yellowhammers are attracted both by barley spilled or thrown in the yard to feed the hens, and by straw bales, where some few odd grains of cereals will still be present and perhaps fall to the ground where the bales are handled. In severe weather birds will shelter in the barn and the cattle court, searching for grain and insects. Where they become used to a regular food supply, such as poultry corn, or grains amongst straw, or residue from the feed for cattle and

sheep, many birds will take advantage of these and visit regularly. Moorhens, or waterhens, are regular visitors to the place we feed our ducks, and an occasional pheasant takes advantage of the hen feeding places. Less welcome are the ubiquitous rats that infest even remote farms, attracted by the supply of food and the presence of poultry and their food. Rooks and jackdaws can be a nuisance with their raiding of poultry and sheep feed. All members of the crow family are daring opportunists. In wilder and high parts of the country with few or no arable fields rooks and jackdaws are not present, but carrion crows are and in the north and west these are replaced by hoodie crows and ravens.

Often the bare hillsides appear to be empty of wildlife, especially in winter, but a close examination can reveal that there is a surprisingly large population of a variety of creatures living in the sparse cover on the ground. On the rather bleak-looking wet, peaty moorlands of the hills in the north a search can reveal the obvious presence of a considerable number of mice or voles, with the evidence of holes and nests. Frogs are quite often seen on the hill, and large numbers of big, black slugs are present. Substantial numbers of insects of many kinds abound, and it is clear that the hills actually sustain a significant variety of wildlife of various types.

Some of the drier, heathery hills in Scotland support huge numbers of blue mountain hares, which turn white in winter, and where roads pass through such country the carcases of these animals killed by motor cars are quite common, in turn providing food for crows, buzzards, stoats and so on. These hares are particularly attracted to areas where new roads have been made and new grass is growing on the freshly made verges. The blue, or white, hares descend upon these roadside verges in numbers at night to feed on the sweet, new grass. Large numbers of hares are unpopular with sheep farmers because of course they compete for the available food with the sheep. These blue mountain hares rarely come into arable fields, and are replaced there by the larger brown hare, though sadly the latter have shown a very marked decline in numbers in many areas in the past twenty years and in a lot of places have become rare. The reason for this is not fully understood. Modern agricultural methods are possibly to blame, and perhaps the early cutting of silage, as opposed to the later cutting of hay, has killed many leverets. Chemical sprays may have had an adverse effect upon the brown hare population too, though there are still places where they are present despite intensive agriculture. The wetter hills, with sparse cover, support few hares or rabbits. Surprisingly perhaps, some hill areas in the far north and west, with wet, peaty, open hills carry a significant badger population, which is an indication of an abundant supply of insects and small creatures, as well as suitable plants and roots, for these omnivores. Badger tracks can be found on paths right out on the hill ground. In many places in the north and west of Scotland there is a flourishing pine marten population too, these animals being less rare than some people might suppose, and spreading their territory, though still localized.

Contrary to what their name might suggest, the pine marten is not merely a creature inhabiting pine forests, but rather lives mostly in areas with rocks and short cover. In a number of places in northern Scotland pine martens are a menace to poultry, stealing both eggs and the birds themselves, particularly hens sitting on nests.

The weather is of considerable importance to those who work on the land or who live in the countryside. It affects everybody, of course, but has significantly less influence upon the lives of those that live and work in towns and cities inside buildings. Farmers especially are influenced by the weather throughout the year, with dry periods often affecting their jobs and livelihoods as much as wet and severe weather. However, whereas arable farmers in lower country may have their work stopped by wet or stormy weather, hill farmers may actually have their work increased by such conditions. When the weather is bad, with heavy rain, or snowstorms, the hill farmers and shepherds will need to check their animals, particularly the sheep, to ensure that these have shelter and are safe. Heavy rain, causing sudden spates in rivers and burns, can endanger livestock, sometimes cutting some animals off from the remainder of the flock or preventing them from reaching shelter, or may wash away parts of fences, allowing beasts to wander. Snow drifting in blizzards can be especially dangerous to animals. Although cattle being larger and stronger are better able to cope with such conditions, blizzards can cause the herd to huddle together to shelter behind stone dykes or other cover, and occasionally young calves can get trampled on and snowed over. Sheep instinctively seek shelter behind dykes or rocks or in hollows, but drifting snow often settles in such places more heavily and in severe weather in the hills an unfortunate sheep can easily find itself quickly in snow too deep to enable it to struggle free, and being powerless then to move they can be buried.

Sheep are quite short in the leg and have difficulty in walking through snow that is up to their bellies. Consequently, in bad weather the hill farmer has to go out to try to ensure that his flock is safe. In the wilder hills where the sheep are spread out over large areas it is often impossible for the shepherd to gather all the flock into safer places in the face of sudden severe weather.

The keeping of animals involves responsibilities that are full time. They have to be looked after on a daily basis. In winter cattle have to be fed every day, but even in summer they need to be checked daily to see that all is well, for it is by constantly seeing his charges and being familiar with their habits and idiosyncrasies that the observant stockman can hope to notice signs of anything amiss with the beasts. If sheep are ranging far on an open hill it may not be practical or possible to check all of them on a daily basis, but frequent checking is necessary nevertheless. Consequently the single-handed hill farmer is unable to leave the farm for long periods, because even if he is able to arrange with someone to check the beasts for him in his absence, the person is unlikely to be familar with them and is therefore liable to fail to notice early signs of problems or unusual behaviour. For this reason most single-handed hill farmers are unable to get away for holidays, although in practice most of them probably can neither afford to take holidays, nor wish to do so, since the daily involvement with their animals becomes part of life. For many of them a major worry is the possibility of suffering a debilitating accident, or worse, some incapacitating injury. They cannot afford the luxury of being ill and following the usual advice to rest for recuperation, for however they feel they still have animals that must be fed and checked. A hill farmer cannot ask his wife to telephone his place of employment to say that he is ill and will not be in for work that day, and a doctor's certificate is of little use to him, even if there is a doctor readily available in his area! Some farms in hill country do not even have near neighbours who might be called upon to assist in emergency. Thus the possibility of a broken limb, or an enforced spell in hospital, is a major worry for most stockfarmers.

However, there are compensations for the hill farmer, despite his reward not being financially attractive, and although it is often a lonely life, working alone much of the day. Working with animals can be satisfying , even if at times it can also be aggravating and frustrating. There is pleasure in seeing calves and lambs born safely and growing up, especially in the case of breeding stock that is kept on the farm. Our cows are all home reared and we have known them all their lives, and their mothers before them, and we know them all individually. In many cases we recognize them by the similarity of their looks to their mothers. On fine days working outside, even in winter, can be refreshing, and sometimes even exhilarating on a nice sunny morning with clear air after a mild frost has thawed, with a view of snow-topped hills in the distance and the sparkling river below. Sometimes in the evenings we watch magnificent sunsets, with spectacular changing colours in the west, and often stretching right across the sky above us, far more impressive than those sometimes depicted on holiday brochures. We call these 'chocolate box' skies, because so often they seem almost too spectacular to be real. They are constantly moving and changing, and provide a truly wonderful display of nature's beauty that surpasses anything that can be made by man. These glorious moments compensate for the times when we have to go out into a storm late at night to help a calving cow or rescue a ewe, or the miserable mornings at lambing time when heavy rain driven by a strong easterly wind kills young lambs by causing hypothermia, and soaks and chills the shepherd too.

January

O nce the midwinter holiday period is past the days start to grow noticeably longer as the evenings draw out and the mornings start earlier each day. It is far from midwinter yet for the hill farmer of course, and the worst weather and hungriest time of year for the cattle and sheep are still to come, and it is never a holiday time for him either. It seems a long time ahead until May and the prospect of more clement weather and grass growth resuming. January is usually a month of snow and ice, and cold wet days. Warm weatherproof and waterproof clothing are a necessity for the farmer and shepherd at this season, and often he and his family will need several changes of outerwear available, for donning soaking clothing when going out on the farm again after returning to the house for meals or other reasons is not to be recommended. Snow and ice are often a

considerable problem for the farmer in the hills, and January is the month most likely for such weather conditions to occur, or to commence. Particularly if there have been low temperatures or earlier snowfalls in December and the ground is already cold or frozen, snow is likely to lie longer and ice to be more difficult to thaw. With many night-time temperatures below freezing at this stage of winter, warmer days, with the thermometer registering above freezing level in the daytime and a slow thaw taking place, can result in a gradual build up of ice with refreezing at night; farm tracks and damp parts of the farm can be covered in thick ice that renders it difficult for cattle and sheep to walk, let alone for the farmer to negotiate with his tractor. The cattle and sheep, especially the latter, become wise to ice and very reluctant to walk upon it. Such conditions can render the taking of the daily feed to the beasts difficult and time consuming, and even dangerous at times. In particularly severe weather, where the ground is covered in deep or frozen snow, or in ice, making it difficult for cattle and sheep to forage for rough grazing, it may well be necessary for the farmer to give extra rations of feed to the livestock, and the problems caused by snow and ice can result in the distribution of feed to the cattle and sheep occupying the whole day. This can also make worrying inroads into the winter feed stockpile at this time of the year, with much of the winter and bad weather still to come.

Some sheep, especially those of hardy hill breeds, are occasionally reluctant to eat hay and prefer to scrape amongst the snow for green matter of some sort underneath and to stay on the higher ground. It may be necessary for the shepherd to struggle through snow to round up these reluctant sheep to bring them down to the feeding areas to try to encourage them to eat feed provided, in order to maintain their condition as well as possible. Some sheep refuse to eat the hay even when it is placed in front of them, or if they are brought to it and kept beside it. In these cases there is little the farmer can do but trust that they can obtain enough food from nibbling twigs and scraping under the snow, in the knowledge that animals generally adapt themselves according to circumstances, and if they were really hungry they would probably eat the feed provided readily enough. Young sheep, gimmers and hoggs, are particularly inclined to be slow in coming to man-provided food until they get used to it and realize the advantage.

Snow renders getting about the farm more difficult, and it has to be cleared from pathways to the house and steading, not merely to save it being brought into the buildings on feet, but because snow compacted by people walking upon it can quickly turn to slippery ice, which can be difficult to walk on, and even dangerous. Often the road to the farm has to be cleared of snow too, in order to allow motor vehicles access. Most hill farms have snowploughs that can be attached to the hydraulic lift arms on the back of the tractor. The farmer can then use his snowplough to clear the road by driving the tractor along it in reverse, pushing the snow out of the way. In deep snow it may be advisable to clear an area for the sheep with the snowplough, where they can feed without tramping through snow up to their chests, or worse. All this extra work takes time, and is a tiring nuisance to the hill farmer. However, ice and extreme cold may often be even more of a nuisance, with outside taps, byre water supplies, and sometimes even the burns freezing up. Beasts need daily water, and if their usual drinking place is frozen, this has to be thawed out, or the ice broken to ensure that they have access to it. Thawing out frozen pipes in a cold byre or steading can be a difficult task, and in very cold weather it is often a losing battle, ending finally in the necessity of carting buckets of water from the house until the thaw comes.

In very cold weather the freezing temperatures may also cause great difficulties for the farmer in starting vehicles. At a temperature of 0°C the power of a battery can drop by 35 per cent. This means that the starter battery for a tractor may have not much more than half power in very cold weather, so that any battery not in good condition may simply not have enough energy to turn over the tractor sufficiently to start it properly. At -18°C the battery power drops to only 40 per cent of normal summer level, and even without other problems this may not be sufficient to start the tractor. Furthermore, at temperatures of perhaps -12°C or so the diesel fuel may start to gel, and the viscous fluid sticks in the filter and starves the engine. Some winter diesel contains an additive to combat this, but it does not always work in very low temperatures, since it is not economic to treat all the diesel with sufficient additive when such low temperatures may occur for only a few days each year. If the farmer is unable to start his tractor to take hay to hungry cattle and sheep the situation can be very serious. In countries such as Canada and Scandinavia where such adverse low temperatures occur for a significant time each winter precautions to cater for these conditions are quite normal. Vehicles in Canada have heaters in the water system that can be plugged into the mains electricity supply heat up the water in the cooling system pipes and so warm the engine block. Having learned from the experience of being unable to get the tractor started, despite trying to warm the engine with copious kettles full of boiling water, we managed to obtain one of these heaters from Canada and installed it in our tractor, and in cold weather this is plugged into the mains on a time switch so that the tractor is warmed up sufficiently by the time that it is required in the morning and starts quite readily. This is then one less worry and hindrance in freezing conditions.

The cold weather of winter is a difficult time for many wild creatures. Some, such as stoats and foxes, may find plenty of rabbits to eat. Others, such as the rabbits themselves, may have difficulty in finding food. The colour of the stoat's fur will turn white overnight at this time of year with a fall of snow, or even after a very heavy white hoar frost. Earlier in the winter one can see brown stoats running along stone dykes or across the corners of fields, or darting across the farm tracks, even after white frosts and falls of snow, but after the end of the year they turn colour overnight to match the white environment. This would seem to indicate that the change of coat colour is dictated not merely by the white environment or the low temperature alone, but also by the factor of daylight length. Once turned white the stoats remain this colour until they shed their winter coats in the spring. We see white stoats frequently, looking absurdly conspicuous with their bright white pelts and black tail ends after the snow has gone. An artist friend once described the black tail tip of an ermine as looking like a fly chasing the stoat through the snow! They are charming animals that, on balance, are of much benefit to the farmer in reducing the rabbit and rat populations. The mechanism of coat colour change appears to vary in different areas and countries, and with different animals. The blue mountain hare changes its coat to white much earlier in winter than stoats, perhaps influenced less by daylight factors. In southern parts of Britain white stoats, or ermines, are comparatively unusual even in late snow, but in the north they are a common sight in most winters.

One evening, returning home along the farm track, I spotted a grey animal behaving oddly at the edge of the hill a few yards ahead. It had a white stripe on its back and at first I thought that it was an injured cat. When I was about thirty yards away from it I realized that it was an ermine on the back of a rabbit with its

teeth fastened upon the back of its victim's neck. The rabbit tottered about for a few minutes before finally collapsing about ten yards away from where I stood quite still. The white stoat let go its hold and stood beside the rabbit, but this still gave a few kicks, and when it did so the stoat grabbed it again briefly. Finally the ermine settled down to have its meal of blood and flesh just in front of me. Every now and again he (for I believe that from its small size it was a young male – the male stoat is smaller and grows more slowly over the first winter than the female) looked up at me, with his little white face red with blood. Twice he wiped his face on the grass. Finally he had had enough to eat, and of me standing there, and retired into some rocks nearby. I had thought that I could see the rabbit still breathing, so I went forward to check, and found that this was in fact so. Despite a significant amount of flesh eaten away at the back of its neck the rabbit was still breathing. I realized then that if the stoat wished to drink the warm blood of the rabbit he would not kill his victim first, because when an animal is dead the blood ceases to flow and it would not bleed properly. Dead animals do not bleed. It occurred to me then that perhaps lions and leopards and other carnivores act in the same way. Certainly my experience of ferrets confirms that these like to lick blood if there is an opportunity to lap it when warm. Dogs do so too if given the opportunity. So it is likely that the big cats also follow suit. Thus it occurred to me that their characteristic throttling the victim by grabbing its throat in their jaws may merely comatose the prey, or render it unconscious, as did the ermine with its victim, only in this case he fastened upon the back of the rabbit's head. I was able to approach the rabbit and examine the result of the stoat's attack, which I had watched for half an hour without disturbing it. I do not suppose that researchers have driven lions off a fresh kill to check whether the animal was actually still bleeding as they commenced their meal!

One unusual feature of the stoat is that an adult male will mate with a very young female when perhaps she is only three weeks old and still deaf and blind. Incredible as this seems, it has not only been shown to be the case, but moreover it seems that most female stoats in their first winter are found to have been served and give birth to a litter of young in the following spring. Stoats, like roe deer, exhibit delayed implantation, which means that the fertilized egg does not develop for some months, which allows the female to give birth at an appropriate time of year for the survival of her offspring, and development of the embryo thus does not retard her own growth.

Otters sometimes visit hill country, and snow provides a good opportunity for observing signs that one has been visiting the burn. As well as noticing from tracks that an otter has followed the burn upstream, searching for eels or spawning seatrout or salmon, or hunting for rabbits sheltering under tussocks, we also occasionally find where they have enjoyed sliding downhill in the snow when taking a shortcut across the corner of a field where the burn bends. Otters sometimes follow burns right uphill into high ground and then cross the hill to the next valley and follow the streams there back down to the main river. They can travel a considerable distance in a night within their home range. At this time of year there are carcases of dead salmon lying in burns towards the mouths where they flow into rivers. These are fish that have died after spawning, some of them diseased. The fish run up the burn during the night, often a mile or two, in order to spawn in suitable redds, or stony patches where the female lays her eggs, which are then fertilized externally by the male. They then drop back to pools at the mouth of the burn, and one can see dead fish lying in the water. The otters eat quite a number of these, sometimes leaving them on the bank where the remains are then accessible to other scavengers. In the autumn salmon and sea trout will occasionally run up even very small streams in a search for suitable spawning places, responding to a natural urge. We have quite often had small sea trout in the little burn in our farmyard in late autumn, unfortunately no longer in fit condition to eat. One day I was coming back from feeding cattle in very wet weather when I came across a sea trout of about a pound in weight wriggling about in a puddle in the middle of the farm track! Because of very heavy rain the hill was sodden and flowing with water, which was filling a ditch on one side of the track and overflowing across this into a tiny burn running down the other side, which in turn joined the burn that runs through the farmyard. The fish had obviously followed the flowing water and diverted up the trickle across the road, presumably in the hope of finding deeper water once through these 'shallows'. I picked it up and returned it to the stream, but doubted that it would survive long anyway. We often see a salmon in the larger burn that runs through the fields on the low side of the farm, but there are very few pools in this for them to lie, so mostly they drop back to the pools near the mouth. On rare occasions a salmon has run up the little burn into our farmyard, and one day my wife nearly tripped over one in the shallow ford when she went to fetch the house cow in the field across the other side to bring her in for milking in the early morning.

Mole activity becomes more evident in hard weather. These animals remain active throughout the winter, requiring to eat large numbers of earthworms to maintain their metabolism. When the ground is frozen they may need to excavate more tunnels lower down because worms and other soil insects drop lower into the ground away from the colder temperatures on the surface, but the soil from these new tunnels has to be removed, and so is pushed upwards. New molehills of freshly pushed up soil are very obvious in frozen or snowy ground, and it is this change in the tunnel system brought about by lower temperatures that causes what seems to be a flurry of mole activity. The number of molehills is actually no guide to the mole population in an area, and the appearance of a lot of molehills in a field indicates the activity of the resident mole in that part of the field, depending upon the size of its territory. The strength of these small animals in being able to dig, and to push all this soil up to the surface through the frozen crust is astonishing. Moles are solitary and aggressive animals and will fight other

moles that trespass into their territories, except for males and females meeting briefly during their mating period. They need to drink, and generally one of their tunnels runs to water somewhere in their territory. Their tunnelling is not a permanent mining in quest for food, but rather they maintain underground tunnel systems, preying upon worms and other creatures that drop into these tunnels. Moles are not totally blind and have small eyes, about 1mm in diameter, which probably enables them to distinguish at least between light and dark; however, they have a keen sense of smell, and with their long noses and sensitive whiskers they are aware of anything entering their tunnel systems, which they patrol regularly. They also store live worms as a reserve food supply, biting the worm to paralyse but not kill it.

Moles are not popular with farmers, for they damage the fields. In areas sown with crops their tunnels undermine seedlings and kill these or interfere with their growth. In grassland the molehills, even when rolled flat, produce bare patches of soil where weed seeds germinate, and stones brought to the surface with these will blunt mower blades at hay time. In silage fields the soil from molehills may be picked up with the cut grass, and this contaminates the silage, which can become toxic to beasts as a result. Moles can be found far out on the hills, and it is amazing to come across fresh molehills in green patches of land surrounding long derelict remains of ancient houses or crofts in remote areas, separated from other better quality soil by miles of acid, peaty ground that would appear to be completely unsuitable for moles and through which one would have thought it most unlikely that they would travel. Moles are actually woodland dwellers too, but there the activity is less apparent in the leaf mould. They are not long-lived animals and it is thought that their average life span is only about two years, with many not surviving more than a year. Owls, herons, buzzards and foxes will all kill and eat moles, and cats will kill them too, but the latter usually leave them and do not eat them. Drought, and a shortage of food, kills off a lot of moles, and of course man is a major predator; although the traditional mole-catchers, who made a living going round farms ridding them temporarily of a surplus of mole activities, exist no longer. Young moles are born in about June or July in high country in the north, but a little earlier in the year further south. There are generally about four young in the family, and they stay in the nest about five weeks, being born naked and relying upon their mother for warmth for the first two weeks until their fur grows, They are entirely dependent upon their mother's milk for the first month, but after about five weeks start to forage in the tunnel system, and after nine weeks they disperse to establish their own territories, probably encouraged by their mother starting to be aggressive towards them.

Moles have a voracious appetite, needing to eat the equivalent of about half their body weight daily to survive. Sometimes they will emerge to search the surface for earthworms after a shower in a dry spell of weather. One day in a dry period in the middle of summer my dogs showed interest in a container of grit for hens in our yard, and picking this up I discovered a mole below it, presumably attracted by the damper ground, and so the possibility of worms, below this. The creature tried to burrow away, which they can do with amazing speed in soft ground, but was unable to do so in the hard farmyard, so I caught it and placed it temporarily in a large glass container so that I could look at it . Out of curiosity I decided to test its reaction with a worm, so I dug up a few in a wet area below a water trough, and dropped one into the container beside the mole. It immediately seized the worm, turned it round the correct way – I suppose head first, perhaps because of the bristles on the worms – and holding it with both front hand-like feet gobbled it down, very audibly, like a monster piece of spaghetti, apparently cleaning the soil from the worm with its hands as it did so. I fed the mole a number of worms, which it ate almost as fast as I could supply them, before I released the animal into more suitable ground.

In frosty conditions outside work such as fencing is impeded, but if the ground is also dry, and there is a breeze from a suitable direction, conditions may be right for the farmer or shepherd to carry out some burning of gorse, grass or heather. In the case of gorse the purpose of burning is to get rid of it. In fact burning gorse only kills the part of the bushes above ground and usually the plant regenerates in time and regrows. However, this gives a period when the grass around the dead gorse bushes can grow unshaded, and provide more grazing for stock. The burned debris adds minerals to the soil. Cattle like eating freshly burned gorse too, probably obtaining minerals from the blackened tips of the bushes, which they seem to relish nibbling. Grass and heather are burned to rejuvenate them and not to kill them, though. Long dead grass, and other herbage, smothers the new leaves that grow in spring, and so burning off this debris assists the new growth, as well as providing minerals from the burned vegetation. The same applies to heather, which benefits greatly from being burned, or heavily grazed, in controlled patches to avoid long, straggly, woody growth. Burning heather in patches and strips, to give a mosaic on the hill of differing levels of growth, is the principle of managing heather moorland for the benefit of grouse, and provides ideal conditions for sheep too, with a variety of stages from succulent young shoots, to older and rather longer heather, available as grazing food in winter. On fine days in hill country, from January onwards, smoke can be seen coming from occasional hill tops, until the advent of the nesting season of the earliest birds, when burning ceases by law. Heather burning is mostly carried out by game-keepers as part of their grouse management, but the farmer may assist too, for the excercise is also beneficial for his sheep. Suitable days with dry conditions are not frequent and advantage has to be taken of them when they present themselves. Gorse in particular seems to burn best after a hard frost. The management of grazing land in this way is not new, and is traditional in many parts of the world, especially in Africa, where indigenous natives have long set fire to grassland to renew grazing and kill parasites.

Although hard winter weather is tiresome at the time, and makes the hill farmer's job more difficult, even without disastrous snowstorms that endanger sheep, and even cattle, there is an old saying that hard weather in winter is good for the beasts. This has some truth in it in that undoubtedly in cold weather cattle and sheep are hungrier and eat more and so probably maintain their condition better, if sufficient food is available. It would also seem that hard weather has an adverse effect upon parasites, and that the result of a mild winter seems to produce less healthy cattle and sheep, with more problems from pneumonia even with calves out on the open hill in spring, and more trouble amongst the sheep from ticks and flystrike.

Rats are a problem on most farms throughout the country, and become especially so in winter when they move into buildings from the surrounding countryside in search not only of food but of more congenial winter accommodation. This is provided by stacks of hay and straw in which they can make warm nests and rear young. During the summer rats live largely out in the fields and hedgerows, frequenting watercourses in particular. Rat holes and runs can be found along burn banks, and burns that run through a farmyard are favoured. Where grain, or bagged feed stored for the winter feeding of cattle and sheep, is kept, this is a great attraction for rats. The damage that these animals can do to the structure of buildings, even including tunnelling through stone-built walls and cement floors, has to be seen to be believed. It is said that where there are mice there are unlikely to be rats, and this seems to be borne out. The rats would

appear to drive away mice. Insofar that we are tolerant of any damage to feedstuffs, we are pleased to see signs of mice in the farm buildings as an indication of no bad infestation of rats. If one has sheep inside a building for adopting lambs, or attending to a sick ewe, or if it is necessary to have a cow inside for a while for some reason, these invariably spill small particles of food, and this attracts rats. Poultry in the farmyard are also certain to attract rats, for food scattered for the hens and ducks will encourage the animals to scavenge for grain, and for any eggs laid in accessible places. Rats are good swimmers, and will dive to retrieve grain thrown into a duck pond. Constant war, with poison and traps, has to be waged against them to minimize damage. We welcome stoats in the farmyard, since they have never interfered with poultry to our knowledge, and do a good job hunting below the hen house or in other places where there is evidence of rat holes. A stoat may steal an odd bantam's egg if it finds a nest without the hen, but we do not grudge this and regard it as deserved reward for the rat hunting. We once watched a stoat with a bantam's egg, which it had found in the garden in front of the house, where the poultry often forage and occasionally nest in the ivy on the dyke. We saw from the window of the house this stoat with the egg, rolling it in front of it along the ground. We watched the animal roll the egg along the bottom of the garden wall, then round the corner and along the side wall for about thirty yards, and finally down half the length of the other end wall where it pushed the egg into the dyke and disappeared with it.

February.

There is an old saying 'If Candlemas (2 February) be fair and bright, winter will have another flight; but if Candlemas be clouds and rain, winter is gone and won't come again!' A more local version is 'If Candlemas be fine and fair, half of winter is to come and mair!' For low-ground farmers February may bring early hope of spring, with daffodils beginning to show in the gardens and a few song birds starting to sing, but for the hill farmer there is much of the long winter to come still at this time of year, and he does well to heed the old saying that 'on Candlemas day' he should have 'locked in the barn half his corn and half his hay!'.

February is perhaps the least pleasant of months for the farmer in the hills. It is about the middle of his winter, when the hills are bare of grazing herbage, if not snow-covered, and although it may not be the busiest time of year – depending upon the weather, and extra work that this may involve – it may be the most worrying. The stockpile of winter feed will be dwindling, and the farmer will be thinking about how many bales of hay and straw he has left in the barn, hoping that there will not be much more severe weather necessitating extra feed for his animals and eating into his reserve supplies of fodder. February and March are known as the 'hungry gap', when the grass has been burned up by the frost and the cold and flattened by the wintry weather, and there are many weeks before signs of new growth will appear, although occasional mild spells can cause tantalizing greening of the grass, especially in damp places. But this flicker of grass growth will not be maintained, for although the days start lengthening rapidly by the middle of February there is a long time to go until daylight length prompts sustained growth. For all the wishful thinking at the start of many seasons that it is going to be an early spring that year, seldom does this occur. Grass does not really start to grow in any sustainable way and show worthwhile growth until at least mid-April, and often the end of April, and there is always a tantalizing period of three weeks at least when the fields and hill begin to look dark green, but there is little more than that and hungry sheep quickly turn the green to bare brown again. As well as warmth and moisture, grass and other herbage need light intensity and appropriate day length to stimulate growth.

On some hills the heather will provide coarse fodder for cattle and sheep, but there is little else available for them at this time of year. Those farmers who lamb some ewes as early as March will already be thinking about the forthcoming lambing season, and will start feeding concentrates to these sheep. To supplement the ewe for the heavy drain on her body resources during the last six weeks of pregnancy, when the growth of the embryo lambs accelerates, extra protein and energy will be required. This is provided in the form of protein blocks or molasses-based licks, and pellets with a high protein content. Oats or barley may also be provided for the sheep, but these require to be fed in troughs to avoid wastage, and this is not always easy for hill farmers, especially in wet conditions where the area around the troughs will be churned up into mud by the feet of the sheep, or it may be difficult to find level areas on which to situate the troughs. Thus concentrated feed in the form of pellets or cobs is often more convenient, for these can be spread on clean ground, from which they are readily picked up by the hungry sheep. After the first few days of calling the sheep down to get their food they will soon learn, and they will be waiting in the mornings for the shepherd to appear with their rations, or come running at the sound of the tractor.

The cattle will continue to be fed hay or straw, and the bales may either be put into large 'haiks', containers made of mesh or metal bars, through which the beasts can pull the hay or reach in with their heads, or they may be spread upon the ground, where clean space is available. Most hay and straw is baled in large round bales these days, which involve less handling, since one large round bale may contain the equivalent of perhaps ten small bales. A big bale can be picked up by the farmer with his tractor front loader and transported to the feeding area in this manner. If there are small numbers of cattle, as on many hill farms, it may be more economical to feed hay on the ground, if clean land is available, since only ten or so cows can feed at a haik containing a large round bale at a time, and calves running with the cows will not be able to get at this, necessitating a special feeding area for these with a creep gate preventing access by the cows, but allowing the calves to creep underneath the barrier. If a hay bale is unrolled upon the ground, then all the cows and calves can feed at it. Where the tractor has access to the top of sloping ground, the unrolling of bales is greatly facilitated by simply cutting off the strings or unwinding the plastic netting binding the bale and rolling it downhill, with the bale rolling in the reverse direction to that in which it was made, so that the hay unwinds from it as it turns. Unwinding a big bale on flat ground can be laborious, especially if hungry cattle are eagerly trying to help themselves. The disadvantage of big bales for the single-handed farmer is that without the appropriate machinery they are difficult to handle because they are so large and heavy. The person with a small hill farm is unlikely to be able to afford duplicate handling machinery, and should his tractor or front loader break down there will be a considerable problem for him in getting big straw or hay bales out onto the hill for feeding his beasts, whereas small bales are easy to handle and carry, and can readily be loaded into a cart or even into a Landrover for transport.

Big bales are not so satisfactory as small ones for feeding sheep unless the flock is a large one, because, apart from the feeding quality factor, big bales have to be fed to sheep in large haiks. If a bale is unrolled on the ground the sheep walk all over the hay, and are fussier than cattle about the fodder they eat and will not consume the hay on which they have walked and so waste a great deal. Since not a great number of sheep can feed simultaneously at a big bale haik, it will be necessary to use a number of these to ensure that the flock is fairly fed. It is usually more practical to feed sheep in a haik off the ground, where not too much hay can get pulled out at once and wasted; sheep are fussy and will only eat good quality leafy hay, ignoring the stemmy parts. Long haiks made from sheep netting to form a sort of cradle to hold the hay, strung to poles or to a fence, often serves the purpose well.

Some farmers may start their spring calving in March, but others may leave this, by varying the date when the bull is run with the cows, until a little later in spring when the weather is kinder. When the bull is left running with the cows all year they generally calve at much the same sort of time of year annually, since cows take some time to recover condition and come into season again after parturition, especially with early spring calving, when their condition may be lower after the winter. Other than maintaining the cows in satisfactory condition, which is neither too fat to render calving more difficult or too lean such that the growth of the calf strains the body reserves of the cow too much, there are no special procedures that have to be observed by the farmer, although there is always the constant necessity for checking daily that all is well with the animals.

However, the sheep will require attention ahead of lambing as well as extra feed. Sheep are susceptible to a wide range of diseases, especially when they are run on land that has carried sheep for a long time and where they are present in large numbers. They carry many parasites, and these are shed on the ground, often in egg form through faeces as in the case with worms that affect the alimentary tract, and become ingested by other sheep. In the same way organisms that cause disease can spread amongst the flock. For this reason it may be necessary to dose sheep regularly, particularly in the case of large flocks where there is not available adequate clean land that has not carried sheep for a year. Where animals are kept on an extensive system in small numbers their susceptibility to becoming infected is obviously less. A number of diseases can infect new lambs, and one method of safeguarding these is to ensure that the mother ewe passes on antibodies to the lamb in her colostrum, or first milk, which will give the lamb some protection for the first few days of its life. So the shepherd may wish to dose the ewes ahead of lambing for worms and in infected areas for liver fluke as well, to try to ensure that his flock is as healthy as possible in the final stages of pregnancy. He may also wish to inject the sheep with preventive doses for the various clostridial and other diseases to which lambs are susceptible in the early days of their lives, so that the ewes can pass on this temporary protection to their offspring in their colostrum. This has to be done a few weeks before lambing commences, but it is not advisable to dose the sheep for both problems simultaneously and it will be necessary to gather the sheep twice into the pens for this purpose. Handling heavily pregnant ewes has to be done with care, and both operations are carried out well before lambing is due in order to cause minimum upset to the heavily in-lamb sheep.

Many hill farms are badly infested with rabbits, which have now come back in numbers that in some areas compare with the populations before myxomatosis almost wiped out the population. Many younger people will not know what the rabbit population was like in pre- myxomatosis days, for it was over forty years ago, in 1953, that the disease was first introduced into Britain, being spread deliberately to combat the scourge of these pests that were causing immense damage to agricultural crops. In a short time the rabbit population largely vanished, and in many areas the countryside was transformed by their eradication. Areas that had been heavily grazed by rabbits then grew comparatively unchecked and scrub and young trees proliferated without being gnawed or eaten. Woods were planted without the necessity of the heavy cost of protection against rabbits, whilst in other areas some plant and insect species that flourished in the heavily grazed environment suffered from the unchecked growth of the herbage and disappeared. Rabbits vanished entirely from many areas, and even now some parts of the country do not have populations comparable to the period before 1953, despite the increase. Other places, including many hill areas, now have fully as many rabbits again as forty years ago, and these are immensely destructive, resulting in very significant financial loss to farmers and landowners. Many of those blaming deer for the lack of natural tree and scrub regeneration without blaming rabbits as well probably have no recollection of the situation forty years ago when the rabbits disappeared temporarily.

When myxomatosis devastated the rabbit population, killing perhaps as much as 99 per cent of rabbits in many areas, this had a dramatic effect upon many other species of animals, and also of birds. The increase in grass and scrub, no longer eaten down by the rabbits, resulted in a massive proliferation of voles. In turn this precipitated a significant increase in the number of weasels that can breed several litters of young in a year when conditions are favourable, and for which voles and mice are a major food supply. On the other hand stoats, which breed more slowly than weasels, being able to have only one litter of young a year, with delayed implantation, declined considerably in numbers. Although stoats will eat voles and mice, they are less able to pursue these down their holes and tunnels than the smaller weasels, and rabbits form a major part of their diet. With the return of rabbits in increasing numbers the stoat population has increased again consistently over the past few years. The equally noticeable increase in the numbers of predatory birds such as buzzards, as well as carrion-eating corvids such as crows and magpies, will have been assisted by the plentiful

supply of rabbits. All of these birds have now reached population levels that are perhaps already causing concern in some areas.

Stoats are enchanting animals that we see frequently hunting in and out of stone dykes or dashing across the roads. Their pursuit of a rabbit, once they have somehow marked a particular victim, is relentless and they will pursue the unfortunate animal for some distance, following it by scent. The pursued rabbit is seemingly somehow mesmerized by fear of the inevitability, since it never seems to run off at full speed, whereby it could easily outpace any stoat, but lollops along at half speed as if it knows that it is doomed, sometimes squealing before the stoat has even reached it. That this should be so is extraordinary when a number of occasions have been recorded of rabbits attacking stoats. We witnessed a rabbit chasing a stoat round in a small circle in the middle of the farm track one day, and it finally leaped and kicked the stoat, knocking it over. At that point they must have noticed our vehicle and they hurriedly departed in opposite directions. A friend told us how he was walking on the farm past a rabbit warren in a pile of rocks when a stoat ran out of this past him. To his surprise the stoat was immediately followed by a rabbit in hot pursuit, and both ran off across the field out of his sight. On both occasions it might be presumed to be a matter of a strongly maternal rabbit defending young, but of course female rabbits do not appear to show such a strong maternal instinct in their attention to their offspring. Despite the apparent ability of a rabbit to turn the tables on a stoat and become the aggressor on rare occasions, we have observed stoats pursuing and killing rabbits a number of times. It is quite common to find a rabbit lying dead with either a wound on the back of its neck, or, more often with a significant amount of flesh eaten from its neck at the back of its head.

We do not see wildcats often, for they are largely nocturnal, but we do see them from time to time on the hill, and from the frequently seen signs of droppings, tracks in the snow and so on, it would appear that in this area at least they are far less rare than some would suppose. Indeed the large areas of forestry plantations grown up in the past thirty years have provided good habitat and cover, as they have for foxes. One day I watched a wildcat climb over a deer fence surrounding a wood. It did so with ease suggesting regularity. There is dispute about the purity of blood in wildcats resulting from inbreeding with the many feral cats that originate from animals breeding unrestricted on some farms and resorting to living wild. Whatever the facts may be with regard to genetic purity, proper wildcats have an appearance quite different from feral cats, often being much larger, with shorter tails in proportion, with the characteristic black rings – although this coloration occurs in tame and feral cats too – and a leaner shape. There is a regularly used wildcat den on our hill in a rocky area, and a friend has observed kittens playing outside. We see wildcats and their signs from time to time as we go about the hill, and welcome their presence as a factor controlling the ubiquitous rabbit population. Although many keepers maintain that most wildcats in the area are cross bred with feral cats, I believe that there is a significant readily identified wildcat population, distinguished by behaviour as well as by size and appearance.

February, then, is the time for farmers to concentrate upon an attack on the rabbit population before the start of a new breeding season. Shooting by itself will not have a significant effect on rabbit numbers, though it is necessary to reduce those rabbits lying out in cover on the hill. To have a worthwhile effect upon the breeding adults it is necessary to have a thorough attack on all the burrows on the farm, either by gassing, or by ferreting. Not only is such an offensive against the rabbits very time-consuming, and difficult to achieve, but recently any market that there was for rabbits has virtually disappeared and they are of little value at present. A few years ago rabbits commanded a sufficient price at certain times of year to encourage countrymen and young boys to earn a little pocket money by killing rabbits and selling them, but regulations introduced from Europe have meant that this market has evaporated, despite farmed rabbits bred in China and elsewhere fetching good prices sold wrapped in plastic ready for cooking and on sale in supermarkets in the cities.

The early months of the year generally bring storms to the hills, and inevitably these result in damage around the farm, as well as presenting dangers to the livestock. Burns in spate often damage, if not wash away, parts of fences, and fallen trees and branches brought down by gales often wreck these too. The repair of broken fences is an important, and often seemingly

unending, job on a stock farm. However for long periods of winter such maintenance jobs as fencing cannot be carried out except with difficulty, and sometimes not at all, because of frozen ground. In wet weather it may be necessary to try to limit the use of a tractor in fields and on parts of the hill because of damage caused by the tracks. Ruts made by tractors in wet ground can last for many years in grassland. Similarly feeding cattle and sheep on damp ground can cause poaching that will ruin the grazing . Areas of hard accessible ground on the hill where beasts can be fed in winter without poaching damage are of considerable value in this respect.

On still clear days in February birdsong starts to cheer the bleak landscape and remind us of forthcoming spring. Early in the morning as daylight dawns the robin sings, and in warmer weather the mavis, or song thrush, may show his return from more clement winter quarters with a song from the tops of the trees round the farmyard. Starlings chuckle away from the roofs of the farm buildings or from the tree tops or electricity wires. Their repertoire can be impressive, and starlings are extraordinary mimics. Often in coastal areas they copy seagulls, and one in our farmyard repeatedly fools me momentarily into thinking that I hear a curlew before they have actually arrived back onto the farm. However they can be rather a nuisance in buildings as a result of carrying substantial quantities of hay and other nesting material into roof spaces, some of which sometimes falls down inside making a tiresome mess. On fine days at this time of year a few great tits

sing too, reminding one of better times coming in a few weeks time when spring arrives.

The craggy herons, as they are known in this area, often fly over the farmyard, sometimes looking like what one assumes the sinister pterodactyls must have appeared in silhouette. The poultry do not like them overhead and peer suspiciously and furtively at the supposed potential danger. The herons spend less time in the fields now for the frogs and frogspawn in the pools are more attraction for them when the water is unfrozen. Mallard are mostly paired at this time of year, and one often disturbs a pair at a small pond or cattle watering hole, where probably they too were attracted by frogspawn and the various insect life now stirring in the water.

So the hill farmer's year draws to an end and another commences and the wonderful cycle of new life begins again. Soon the daffodils, now showing green shoots above the soil, will be blooming. But we always get snow when the daffodils are out, if only for a couple of days at most, and it is as well to remember that until the middle of April at least one cannot think safely in terms of winter passing, and the feeding of cattle will continue for a further month after that. May to September is the hill farmer's summer, for spring in the higher country tends to be short-lived. Soon the hills will be green again, and ewes with lambs beside them will graze on the new growth, and the cows and calves will be in the fields or lower parts of the hill, and for a month or two the idyllic country scene will present itself to those that drive by in their motor cars, or holiday in hill areas. But the hills are the workplace of the farmers, from which they seek to make a living, as well as their home, and it is well for the tourists and holidaymakers, hillwalkers and picnickers, to remember this as they enjoy the countryside that they visit, and to avoid disturbance with excessive noise, or litter or other signs of human interference; for they come and then they go again, but the shepherds, farmers and other country people live there all their lives, and the cattle and the sheep are their livelihood, and the wild animals and birds that share their environment are a valuable part of it and should not be disturbed but allowed to live in peace. Cattle and sheep recognize strangers and are nervous of them; even when friends accompany us whilst walking on the farm the wariness of the beasts towards unfamiliar figures is obvious. This is even more so when strangers are unaccompanied by familar people and familiar voices. Wild animals are disturbed even more by humans displaying irregular behaviour such as walking in unusual places or wearing brightly coloured clothing, and unthinking visitors to the countryside are often unaware of the disturbance that they unwittingly cause. The countryside may be regarded as being there for the enjoyment of all, to some extent, but those that cause disturbance, whether knowingly or not, are being selfish to both the wildlife that inhabits that environment and to those that live and work there.

SMITH

19